TESTIMONY

C O M P I L E D   B Y

H. STEPHEN STOKER
& JOSEPH C. MUREN

BOOKCRAFT • SALT LAKE CITY, UTAH • 1980

Copyright © 1980 by Bookcraft, Inc.
All rights reserved

Library of Congress Catalog Card Number: 79-56174
ISBN 0-88494-391-7

3 4 5 6 7 8 9 10   89 88 87 86 85 84

Lithographed in the United States of America
PUBLISHERS PRESS
Salt Lake City, Utah

ACKNOWLEDGMENTS

Appreciation is expressed to the following living General Authorities who gave their personal permission for use in this compilation of quotations from their sermons and writings: Spencer W. Kimball, Marion G. Romney, Mark E. Petersen, LeGrand Richards, Howard W. Hunter, Gordon B. Hinckley, Bruce R. McConkie, Franklin D. Richards, Neal A. Maxwell, Marion D. Hanks, Paul H. Dunn, Theodore M. Burton, Robert L. Simpson, O. Leslie Stone, Hartman Rector, Jr., Loren C. Dunn, Eldred G. Smith, Henry D. Taylor, John H. Vandenberg, and S. Dilworth Young.

Appreciation is also expressed to copyright owners for permission to use materials as follows: for quotations from Conference Reports, Area Conference Reports, *Improvement Era*, *New Era*, *Instructor*, *Ensign*, and *Relief Society Magazine*, the Corporation of the President of The Church of Jesus Christ of Latter-day Saints; for quotations from books published by Deseret Book Company, Deseret Book Company; for quotations from Brigham Young University Speeches of the Year, Brigham Young University Press.

KEY TO ABBREVIATIONS

ACR: Area Conference Report

BYU: *Brigham Young University Speeches of the Year*

CN: *Church News*

CR: Conference Report

DD: Neal A. Maxwell, *Deposition of a Disciple*, Salt Lake City; Deseret Book Company, 1976.

DSL: Harold B. Lee, *Decisions for Successful Living*, Salt Lake City; Deseret Book Company, 1973.

DW: *Deseret Weekly*

EN: *Ensign*

ER: John A. Widtsoe, *Evidences and Reconciliations*, Salt Lake City; Bookcraft, Inc., 1960.

FCW: Harold B. Lee, *Father, Consider Your Ways*, Salt Lake City; The Church of Jesus Christ of Latter-day Saints, 1973 (pamphlet).

FL: Mark E. Petersen, *A Faith To Live By*, Salt Lake City; Bookcraft, Inc., 1959.

FPM: Spencer W. Kimball, *Faith Precedes the Miracle*, Salt Lake City; Deseret Book Company, 1972.

GGG: Theodore M. Burton, *God's Greatest Gift*, Salt Lake City; Deseret Book Company, 1976.

HC: Joseph Smith, *History of The Church of Jesus Christ of Latter-day Saints*, Salt Lake City; Deseret News, 1949.

IE: *Improvement Era*

IN: *Instructor*

JI: *Juvenile Instructor*

MD: Charles W. Penrose, *Mormon Doctrine*, Salt Lake City; Juvenile Instructor Office, 1888.

MI: *Messages of Inspiration*, Salt Lake City; Deseret Book Company, 1957.

MJB: *Melvin J. Ballard – Crusader for Righteousness*, Salt Lake City; Bookcraft, Inc., 1966.

MS: *Millennial Star*

MT: Alvin R. Dyer, *The Meaning of Truth*, Salt Lake City; Deseret Book Company, 1961.

NE: *New Era*

RS: *Relief Society Magazine*

SHP: Harold B. Lee, *Stand Ye in Holy Places*, Salt Lake City; Deseret Book Company, 1974.

TC: Alvin R. Dyer, *The Challenge*, Salt Lake City; Deseret Book Company, 1962.

TMH: Orson F. Whitney, *Through Memory's Halls*, Independence, Missouri; Zions Printing and Publishing Company, 1930.

TTC: Neal A. Maxwell, *A Time to Choose*, Salt Lake City; Deseret Book Company, 1975.

UA-CHD: Unpublished address, Church Historical Department

UU: University of Utah Institute of Religion Devotional Address

WPF: Neal A. Maxwell, *Wherefore, Ye Must Press Forward*, Salt Lake City; Deseret Book Company, 1977.

WW: Matthias F. Cowley, *Wilford Woodruff*, Salt Lake City; Bookcraft, Inc., 1964.

CONTENTS

1

WHAT IS A TESTIMONY?

A.   Descriptions of a Testimony

(1A-1) *The power equipment removing boulders from the road.* A sure knowledge of the spiritual is an open door to great rewards and joys unspeakable. To ignore the testimony is to grope in caves of impenetrable darkness, to creep along in fog over hazardous highways. That person is to be pitied who may still be walking in darkness at noonday, who is tripping over obstacles that can be removed, and who dwells in the dim flickering candlelight of insecurity and skepticism when he need not. The spiritual knowledge of truth is the electric light illuminating the cavern; the wind and sun dissipating the fog; the power equipment removing boulders from the road. It is the mansion on the hill replacing the shack in the marshes; the harvester shelving the sickle and cradle; the tractor, train, automobile, and plane displacing the ox team. It is the rich nourishing kernels of corn instead of the husks in the trough. (*Spencer W. Kimball,* FPM, p. 14.)

(1A-2) *An antitoxin against sin.* Sometimes I have thought that testimony, this something which has such a tremendous force and power in the life of a man, is not uncomparable to those antitoxins which science has discovered to procure immunity from disease. I doubt not that but a few years ago if the world had been told that there were ways of warding off yellow fever, typhoid, smallpox and other highly contagious diseases that there would have been general disbelief. Today these are proven facts. The mere injection of a serum into the blood will procure a substantial immunity which has saved the lives of thousands and hundreds of thousands of people from these diseases which once mowed down the human family in great epidemics, as the machine would mow down the ripened grain. May there not be something akin to this in the form of testimony that is injected into the very blood of a man, which wards off the disease of sin and makes a man immune from those microbes that come from the hand of Satan, scattered about among the human family to encourage wrong-doing and departure from the established course of righteousness? I do not know that such a comparison is proper or illuminating, but this I do know, that sin is disease and that testimony of Christ procures immunity from that disease. Not that man is deprived of his agency, but that while he reacts and responds to the great force and power of testimony, disease in the form of sin has no power over him, and into his life there comes a protection against a more dreaded disease than any of those contagions which have been mitigated by the discoveries of science. This protection, this immunity from disease and sin, is open to all. (*Stephen L Richards*, CR, Oct. 1925, p. 118.)

(1A-3) *Key to successful living in all stages of existence.* A testimony of Jesus is the key to successful living. It was so in the spirit world, for those who overcame Satan there did so "by the blood of the Lamb, and by the word of their testimony." (Revelation 12:11.) It is so here in this life, and it will be so in the life to come, for there is no other name given, in heaven or in earth, whereby we must be saved. In one's testimony that Jesus is the Christ, so far as he can do anything about it, resides the power of God unto salvation. (*Marion G. Romney*, BYU, 3 Feb. 1960, p. 9.)

(1A-4) *A motivating, soul-transforming conviction.* When we speak of a testimony of the Gospel, we refer to a motivating, soul-transforming conviction. One may not know how he received the testimony, nor will he be able to give it to another. There is but one source, and it is available to all who comply with the conditions.

A testimony of the Gospel is of inestimable and eternal value. It is predicated upon obedience, as are all blessings from God; and it may be lost through disobedience or sin. (*Hugh B. Brown*, IN, Oct. 1959, p. 320.)

(1A-5) *An anchor to the soul in the midst of confusion and strife.* [A] . . . testimony of the gospel is an anchor to the soul in the midst of confusion and strife. Knowledge of God and his laws means stability, means contentment, means peace, and with that a heart full of love reaching out to our fellow men, offering the same blessings, the same privileges. (*David O. McKay*, CR, Oct. 1960, p. 7.)

(1A-6) *A divine power which lights up men's souls.* This power, known as testimony of the gospel, is one of the most dynamic forces in the world when it comes into a person's heart. It is that divine power which lights up men's souls and gives them deep feelings, indescribable inward peace, unbounded joy, and great understanding. Yes, it endows them even with hidden treasures of knowledge. It guides them back to God. (*Milton R. Hunter*, CR, Oct. 1965, p. 81.)

(1A-7) *A real and tangible transforming force.* I am persuaded that the testimony of Jesus is something indescribable, but nevertheless some real tangible thing that has force and power, something which serves, when once taken into the structure of a man's life, to work therein a transformation, to change some of the vital elements which are part and parcel of his life.

Great physical forces themselves defy the efforts of science to fully describe and comprehend them. Science has not given the constituency of gravity. What is light? What is electricity? What is heat? As I understand it, we know these great forces of nature only by the effects which they produce. We see their manifestations and we conclude that they exist, but can we describe them? I believe that with all the advancement made in the processes of scientific research and investigation they are yet mysteries to the intelligence of man. It is unthinkable that just as light, heat and gravity are great forces of nature, bringing to bear upon the whole universe the results and manifestations of their power, that there may be in the world of men a force somewhat comparable, coming from God, which takes lodgment in the very beings of men and there brings about these transformations, these remarkable manifestations, not at all incomparable with those manifestations that come from the operation of the physical forces. (*Stephen L Richards*, CR, Oct. 1925, p. 117.)

(1A-8) *The power that binds man and God together.* What is testimony? It is the rock of the Church. It is the *power* that binds man and God together, while he sojourns here in this life. It requires the administration of the Holy Ghost to obtain it and requires conformity to gospel principles to keep it. (*Alvin R. Dyer,* MT, pp. 117-118.)

(1A-9) *Heart-knowledge, the strongest and most direct evidence of truth.* The truth of the Gospel comes to the heart as well as to the understanding. This heart-knowledge or testimony of the Gospel is, after all, to each individual who has it, the strongest and most direct evidence of the truth of the Gospel. To a life in close communion with God and therefore in harmony with His laws this testimony daily grows clearer and stronger. (*Charles A. Callis,* CN, 16 Sept. 1944, p. 11.)

(1A-10) *A personal revelation from God.* Everyone of you who has a testimony and bears it is telling about a personal revelation from God. It is nothing less, or it isn't a testimony, because the Holy Ghost revealed it to you. If you have a testimony, it is a revelation. (*Spencer W. Kimball,* UA-CHD, 2 Jan. 1959 — Los Angeles, Calif., p. 14.)

(1A-11) *The thing which gives us the power to endure.* A testimony is the thing which gives us the power to endure, endure the scoffs and the ridicule that are sometimes heaped upon us, and to endure likewise the praise which comes to us and about us, endure praise so that we may not be turned aside and become proud, boastful, and haughty in our attitudes and spirits. (*J. Reuben Clark, Jr.,* IE, Aug. 1949, p. 495.)

(1A-12) *The greatest comfort that can come to a human heart.* A firm testimony of Jesus is the greatest comfort which may come to the human heart. There is a great need for that comfort today and greater need will arise as we endure more of the sacrifices and deprivations that this terrible war is bringing. There will be scarcely a family that has not someone in danger, and the cold hand of death will reach into many a home and take away loved ones whose companionship is more precious than anything else in life. In such cases the kindly ministrations of friends and neighbors will help, but neither they nor anything else can bring the comfort, the lasting consolation, and the hope that come from a sure testimony in the reality of spiritual life and the immortality of the soul of man. Wives who lose husbands and mothers who lose their sons want to know that they are not gone forever and that they will meet them again, and the only place in the wide world they can obtain that blessed assurance is in the testimony of Jesus and His holy gospel.

What a boon it would be to every soldier facing death either on the vast expanses of the ocean or in the battlefields of the jungle, the desert, the mountain, or the plain, to know deep down in his heart, with a conviction beyond question, that the Savior of the world is his Lord and King, that He gave His own life to make life everlasting, and that whatever happens, a good man will not ultimately lose his life, but will find it! (*Stephen L Richards*, CN, 16 Jan. 1943, p. 7.)

(1A-13) *Commitment to a course of conduct.* To say that one has a testimony of the gospel is to indicate that something has happened in his lifetime that has committed him to a course of conduct which, if he has courage, fortitude, and faith enough, will eventuate in his eternal salvation. (*Hugh B. Brown*, BYU, 2 May 1972, p. 1.)

(1A-14) *A sacred gift.* A testimony is a sacred gift. It is not to be trifled with; it is not a matter to be boasted about; it is a matter to be treated in the greatest humility, to be used whenever the cause of the Lord requires it to be used, to be cherished, nurtured, fed by righteous living. (*J. Reuben Clark, Jr.*, IE, Aug. 1949, p. 495.)

(1A-15) *The highest type of knowledge.* A testimony is a statement of certainty of belief in the gospel of Jesus Christ. It is the highest type of knowledge. It comes as a revelation when truth is known and obeyed. It is the product of harmony with law. Once obtained, it explains the purpose of life; it lightens the duties of the day; and it gives zest to life. It is really man's chief possession. (*John A. Widtsoe*, IE, May 1945, p. 273.)

B.   Essential Components of a Testimony

(1B-1) *Aspects of a living testimony.* There are many types of testimonies and testimonies to many things. The testimony I have in mind . . . is an abiding, living, moving conviction of the truths revealed in the gospel of Jesus Christ.

One aspect of such a testimony is a settled conviction that there is a personal God — "an exalted man" was the phrase the Prophet Joseph used in describing him — and that he is our Heavenly Father. A second aspect of such a testimony is a belief in God's plan of salvation, with Jesus Christ as the central figure. Another essential aspect to such a testimony is a belief in the Prophet's account of his first vision: that in it he saw God, our Eternal Father, and Jesus Christ, His Son, that they stood before him and conversed with him, and that he conversed with them.

Still another requisite is an acceptance of the fact that the Book of Mormon came forth in the manner that the Prophet Joseph said it came forth, that Moroni delivered to him the plates of gold upon which the ancient record was inscribed, and that he, the Prophet, made the translation by the gift and "power of God." (Doctrine and Covenants 1:29.) One must also be convinced that the Prophet received from heavenly beings all of the principles, ordinances, and priesthood powers required to enable men to gain exaltation in the celestial presence of God and that The Church of Jesus Christ of Latter-day Saints is the repository of such principles, ordinances, and priesthood powers.

One who has such a testimony accepts the truth that the keys to the kingdom of God have been held by every man who has presided over this Church, from the Prophet Joseph to and including our present prophet, President Spencer W. Kimball. One of the most important things about such a testimony, and one of the most difficult to obtain, is a conviction that the living prophet is just as much a prophet as was the Prophet Joseph Smith, Jr.

For some people it is much easier to accept ancient prophets than to accept living prophets. This was true in the days of Jesus. He charged the scribes and Pharisees with being hypocrites because they built tombs of the dead prophets and killed the living prophets. (See Matthew 23:29-34.) (*Marion G. Romney*, ACR, Aug. 1975 — Tokyo, Japan, pp. 45-46.)

(1B-2) *We mean three things in particular.* When we say we have a testimony of this work, we mean three things in particular: we mean, number one; that we know by the revelations of the Holy Spirit to our souls that Jesus is the Lord, that he was born into the world as the literal Son of God, that he came with the power of immortality because God was his father and he was thereby able to work out the infinite and eternal atoning sacrifice. The atonement of the Lord Jesus is the most important single thing in all revealed religion. The second point in our testimony is that God has in these last days, through the instrumentality primarily of Joseph Smith, restored anew the knowledge of Christ and the knowledge of salvation and given again every key and power and right and prerogative that enables us men to do the things that will save and exalt us in the highest heaven of the celestial world. And the third great truth in a testimony is to know that The Church of Jesus Christ of Latter-day Saints as now constituted with President Spencer W. Kimball as its presiding officer is, in the most literal and real and full sense of the word, the kingdom of God on earth, the only true and living church upon the face of the whole earth, and the one place where salvation is found. (*Bruce R. McConkie*, ACR, Feb. 1976 — Sydney, Australia, p. 17.)

(1B-3) *The mighty facts of which we may bear testimony.* As Latter-day Saints we have a responsibility to bear a particular kind of testimony — all of us. And what is that testimony?

First of all, that God lives, that he is truly our Eternal Father and we are his literal spirit offspring. Second, that Jesus Christ, the Son of God, is the Savior of the world, and that he has a modern ministry as well as an ancient one, and that you and I — all of us — are involved in that modern ministry. Third, that Joseph Smith was raised up in these last days and especially chosen as an instrument through whom the Lord would introduce his modern ministry to the world. And fourth, that following Joseph Smith there has been an unbroken line of prophets who have carried on his work and will continue to do so. These are the mighty facts of which we may bear testimony. (*Mark E. Petersen*, BYU, 1977, p. 195.)

(1B-4) *Three important truths in every effective testimony.* There are three important truths in every effective testimony. First, Jesus Christ is the Son of God, the Savior of the world, the Redeemer of mankind. Second, Joseph Smith was and is a prophet of God called to restore the gospel and kingdom of God upon the earth in these last days to prepare the world for the second coming of Christ. Third, the Church is the only true and living church upon the face of the whole earth with which the Lord is well pleased. (See Doctrine and Covenants 1:30.) (*Delbert L. Stapley*, BYU, 23 Mar. 1971, p. 1.)

2

THE SIGNIFICANCE OF A TESTIMONY

A. Strength of the Church

(2A-1) *This is the secret.* Students of human affairs, theologians and other thinking men have expressed their amazement at the vitality of The Church of Jesus Christ of Latter-day Saints and they say we have some secret for our unprecedented development. Now let me tell you what that secret is. I take you all into confidence. . . . This is the secret. Every member of this Church stands upon his own feet, upon his own testimony, upon his own conviction that this is the Church of Jesus Christ. . . . Now, in a great building such as this Tabernacle, one part depends upon the other parts. Knock out one of those columns and that part of the gallery would be endangered. Remove several of them and a section of the balcony would collapse. But suppose that every part of the building rested upon its own foundation. Then the destruction of one part would not affect the others. Now, that is the secret. (*James E. Talmage,* CR, Apr. 1920, p. 104.)

(2A-2) *Strength of the church not in its buildings, chapels, etc.* I would like to say to you, that is the strength of this cause, the individual testimony that lies in the hearts of the people. The strength of this church is not in its buildings, in its chapels, in its offices, in its schools; it is not in its programs or its publications. They are important, but they are only a means to an end, and that end is the building of testimony — a conviction that will weather every storm and stand up to every crisis in the hearts and the lives of the membership. (*Gordon B. Hinckley*, ACR, Aug. 1971 — Manchester, England, pp. 160-161.)

(2A-3) *"Black secret" of Mormonism.* Years ago, when our missionaries were being severely persecuted in England, the English government sent a representative to Utah to study our people. They wanted to know what it was that caused the Church to keep sending its missionaries there when they were being so persecuted. After that individual had spent some time in our midst, he returned to his native land and told them that the black secret of Mormonism was the fact that each member knew he had the truth. Now, isn't that what we ought to have? Isn't that just what Jesus promised — that if you will do the will of the Father, you "shall know of the doctrine, whether it be of God, or whether I speak of myself"? (John 7:17.) (*LeGrand Richards*, CR, Apr. 1968, pp. 120-121.)

(2A-4) *It was not Brigham Young.* On a certain occasion I had a conversation with Dr. Frederick L. Paxson, chairman of the History Department at the University of California and one of America's outstanding historians. This conversation suggests God's method of transmitting light and knowledge to his children here on earth, and so I shall use it as the basis of my talk today.

Dr. Paxson stated that it was his opinion that Brigham Young was perhaps the greatest colonizer that the world had ever known. He explained that after founding Salt Lake City, Brigham Young sent settlers in every direction from that center, resulting in colonizing an expansive desert country. Dr. Paxson stressed the point that wherever President Young told his followers to go, they went without any hesitation. Then he gave his reasons to account for Brigham's outstanding success as a colonizer.

"Brigham Young," so he explained, "was one of those rare individuals blessed with an exceedingly forceful personality. He was a man naturally endowed with unusual powers of leadership. Through those natural powers of leadership and as a result of his unusual forceful personality, he was able to completely dominate the lives of the Latter-day Saints. Thus his followers always did Brigham's biddings."

After completing his explanation, Dr. Paxson said to me, "Am I not correct, Mr. Hunter, in my appraisal of Brigham Young, and are not these the reasons why he was so successful in colonizing such a vast empire in the great West?"

I replied: "No, Dr. Paxson, in my opinion the reasons you gave are not the most vital factors which caused the Mormon leader to do such an outstanding job as a colonizer. I do agree that he possessed the powers of personality and leadership that you described, but there is another factor far more important than anything that you mentioned which completely dominated the lives of Brigham Young and his people.

"The supreme reason Brigham Young and all the Saints migrated to Utah was that each of them had in his heart a burning testimony of the truthfulness of the restored gospel of Jesus Christ. Each one accepted without any mental reservation the reality of the existence of God the Father and Christ the Son and felt a close personal relationship to them. It was a positive fact to each Latter-day Saint that the Eternal Father and his only Begotten Son had appeared to Joseph Smith in the Sacred Grove, and also that other heavenly beings had appeared to the Prophet and given to him the priesthood through which he had organized the true Church of Jesus Christ. They firmly maintained that all the principles and ordinances of the gospel which had been on earth in former dispensations were revealed from heaven to the Prophet Joseph. Thus, Brigham Young and his followers maintained that Joseph had been God's mouthpiece here upon the earth — his holy prophet, seer, and revelator — just as literally as had any of the Old Testament prophets.

"Following the martyrdom of Joseph Smith, the members of the Church who migrated to Utah maintained that all the power and authority from God which had been brought by heavenly beings to Joseph had been bestowed upon his successor, Brigham Young. The Saints were positive that their pioneer leader was now God's holy anointed prophet, seer, and revelator. His word was accepted, therefore, as the word and the will of the Lord. The Saints firmly believed that they with Brigham were building the kingdom of God under divine direction from heaven.

"Thus, Dr. Paxson," I concluded, "an individual testimony of the gospel of Jesus Christ possessed by each Latter-day Saint was actually the dynamic force which caused Brigham Young and his followers to withstand mob violence and terrible persecutions in the East, to leave

their homes and comforts of life, and to willingly suffer untold
hardships, hunger, disease, and — for many of them — death, and
endure numerous other difficulties encountered in making more than a
thousand miles' trek through the wilderness to their promised land.
Their positive, dynamic testimonies caused thousands of people to
follow Brigham Young's suggestions, obey his instructions and com-
mands, and successfully make 'the desert . . . blossom as the rose.' "
(Isaiah 35:1.) (*Milton R. Hunter,* CR, Oct. 1965, pp. 80-81.)

(2A-5) *Wherein lies the secret of the Church's vitality?* Many people today
wonder wherein lies the secret of the growth, stability, and vitality of
The Church of Jesus Christ of Latter-day Saints. The secret lies in the
testimony, possessed by each individual who is faithful in the Church,
that the gospel consists of correct principles. It is that same testimony
that was given to Peter and to others in the primitive Church.

This testimony is revealed to every sincere man and woman who
conforms to the principles of the gospel of Jesus Christ, who obeys the
ordinances, and who becomes entitled to receive, and does receive, the
Holy Ghost to guide him. (*David O. McKay,* IE, Feb. 1967, p. 2.)

(2A-6) *The Church is built on testimony.* The restored Church of our Lord
is built upon . . . the individual testimonies of its members. Indeed no
one is asked to come into the Church until he has personal assurance of
the divine truth it teaches. At times it is something of a shock to
applicants for admission into the Church to be advised that the evidences of their real conversion are not adequate. Such persons are not
infrequently urged to further investigation and more supplication that
they may know of a surety that it is the truth which they embrace.

A young lawyer once told me that he would like to join our Church. I
knew him to be a fine fellow and I told him we would be glad to have
him as a member. I told him also that it was necessary to do something
more than merely to indicate his desire for membership. I advised him
that he should make careful study of the gospel, that the principles
taught by the Church would seem reasonable and desirable to him but
that that was not enough. I then told him that in his studies he would be
expected to supplicate the Lord for a divine impression of the truth and
divinity of the work, which we call a testimony. He was much surprised
and I think disappointed. He said he had assumed that all that was
necessary was a willingness to join. He did not know that the true

disciples of Christ are they who have no doubt as to His divinity and His Lordship. (*Stephen L Richards*, CN, 16 Jan. 1943, p. 7.)

(2A-7) *The strength of the Church not in money paid as tithing.* The strength of this Church is not to be measured by the amount of money paid as tithing by the faithful members, nor by the total membership of the Church, nor by the number of chapels or temple buildings. The real strength of the Church is measured by the individual testimonies to be found in the total membership of the Church. (*Harold B. Lee*, ACR, Aug. 1972 — Mexico City, Mexico, p. 117.)

(2A-8) *We are only a handful: testimony is our strength.* We know that Joseph Smith's testimony is true; we know it by the Holy Ghost; and that is the strength of this Church. It is not the sagacity of its leaders, it is not its members, that constitutes its strength. We are only a handful in the midst of millions. The strength of this Church is in the testimony possessed by every man and woman belonging to it, that it is indeed the work of God. (*Orson F. Whitney*, CR, Apr. 1914, p. 41.)

B.   Benefits a Testimony Brings

(2B-1) *The fruits of a true testimony: high ideals.* High ideals and standards of living are the fruits of a true testimony. From the moment one is gained, we start to grow and advance. A testimony motivates us to action. It brings about a change in our hearts and lives. It instills and impels a desire to be an example and an inspiration to others. A testimony brings peace — a calm assurance — and it encourages us to conduct ourselves righteously and give kindly attentions to our loved ones and all of our Heavenly Father's children. (*Delbert L. Stapley*, BYU, 23 Mar. 1971, p. 4.)

(2B-2) *Walking above the things of the world.* That is what I think a testimony is for, to guide and direct us to do the things that will bring us true joy and happiness. If you apply this in your own lives, you will know how wonderful it is when your testimony is such that it enables you to walk above the things of the world, and the weaknesses and wickedness of the world, so that you can look all men in the face and fear no man because you are walking in the ways of the Lord and keeping His commandments. (*LeGrand Richards*, BYU, 10 May 1955, p. 5.)

(2B-3) *It enables one to pass through the dark valley of slander.* If you have that testimony of truth on your side, you can pass through the dark valley of slander, misrepresentation, and abuse, undaunted as though you wore a magic suit of mail, that no bullet could enter, no arrow could pierce. You can hold your head high, toss it fearlessly and defiantly, look every man calmly and unflinchingly in the eye, as though you rode, a victorious king returning at the head of your legions, with banners waving and lances glistening and bugles filling the air with music. (*David O. McKay*, CR, Apr. 1958, p. 130.)

(2B-4) *A shield against the fiery darts of the adversary.* Of what value is a testimony of the gospel of Jesus Christ? It is of much value, because it is the only plan of life that will bring us happiness, tranquility of spirit, and understanding. It also keeps us striving unabatedly and eternally for perfection of soul. It is the strongest shield one can have against the fiery darts of the adversary. (*Delbert L. Stapley*, BYU, 23 May 1971, pp. 3-4.)

(2B-5) *A testimony leads to revelation in other fields.* Well, now, if anyone has a testimony, that means that he has managed to that extent to get in tune with the revelations of the Spirit, and consequently he has received knowledge from a Divine Source of the truth and divinity of the work. If you can get in tune with the Lord and have a testimony of the divinity of this work, then you can comply and conform with the same law that entitles you and enables you to get inspiration and knowledge in other fields; you can learn what you ought to do in your Church affairs, in your school affairs, and in your personal affairs. You can learn whom you should marry, what job you should take, whom you should associate with, and where you should go, whether you should accept a call to missionary service, or whatever it may be. (*Bruce R. McConkie*, BYU, 29 Sept. 1964, p. 7.)

(2B-6) *Requirements become challenges rather than burdens.* As President Lee indicated yesterday, the strength of this church lies in the hearts of its people, in the individual testimony and conviction of the truth of this work. When an individual has that witness and testimony, the requirements of the Church become challenges rather than burdens. Declared the Savior: " . . . my yoke is easy, and my burden is light." (Matthew 11:30.) (*Gordon B. Hinckley*, CR, Apr. 1973, p. 74.)

(2B-7) *Eternal hope and a heavenly monitor.* A personal testimony is and ever will be the strength of the Church. Happy the man in whose soul this unwavering, rocklike power abides, for he has eternal hope and a heavenly monitor that will dwell in him here and hereafter.

The power of a testimony is measured by what the bearer of the testimony of Jesus Christ is willing and ready to suffer for it. (*Charles A. Callis*, IE, Aug. 1945, p. 487.)

C.   Relative Value of a Testimony

(2C-1) *The most precious of all possessions.* There are some people in the world today . . . who know that God is their father and that he is not far from them. If they were to speak on the subject, they would tell you that of all their possessions this knowledge is the most precious. From it they obtain power to resist temptation, courage in times of danger, companionship in hours of loneliness, and comfort in sorrow. This knowledge of God gives them faith and hope that tomorrow will be better than today. It is an anchor to their souls which gives purpose to life, though all men and things about them be in confusion and chaos. They know that such conditions have come because men are without that knowledge and are therefore not guided by God. (*Marion G. Romney*, EN, Aug. 1976, p. 4.)

(2C-2) *A possession more valuable than sight.* Some time ago a lovely sister in the Church came to see me. Though she was blind from birth, she was a convert to the Church through the missionary program. She had two sisters, but she was the only one in her family who had accepted the gospel. She said she wouldn't trade places with her sisters for anything. When I asked her why not, she said, "They have their sight and I don't, but they cannot see." Then she bore testimony to me that she knew God lives, that Jesus is the Christ, that Joseph Smith was a prophet of God, and that the gospel has been restored. This testimony was more valuable to her than anything else, even more than to have her sight. (*Eldred G. Smith*, ACR, Aug. 1973 — Munich, Germany, p. 9.)

(2C-3) *The most valuable thing in the world.* The story is told that there was a new minister who moved into the community where Thomas

Carlyle lived, and he went to the office of Carlyle and asked this question: "What do the people of this community need more than anything else?" And Carlyle's answer was: "They need a man who knows God other than by hearsay."

You know, I have thought a lot about that. I think what this world needs today more than anything else is to know God other than by hearsay. . . .

I would like to say to all those who are within the sound of my voice this day, and who are not members of this Church and do not know the truth of this testimony other than by hearsay: I promise you, as one of his apostles of this dispensation, that if you will study his message and ask God, the Eternal Father, he will manifest the truth of this unto you, and it will be worth more to you than all else in this world. (*LeGrand Richards,* CR, Apr. 1968, pp. 120, 122.)

(2C-4) *I wanted every senator to know.* I picked up volume three of the "Investigation of Reed Smoot," and it opened to page 593. I read these words, which are part of the charges made against me by Mr. Tayler, the prosecuting attorney, I may term him, at that time:

> Several hundred thousand sincere men and women have believed and now believe, as they believe in their own existence, that Joseph Smith, Jr. received revelations direct from God, and if anyone ever believed that we must assume that Senator Smoot believes it. Now a Senator of the United States might believe anything else in the world but that and not be ineligible to a seat in the body to which he belongs. He might believe in polygamy; he might believe that murder was commendable; he might deny the propriety as a rule of life of all the ten commandments; he might believe in the sacrifice of human life; he might believe in no God or in a thousand gods; he might be Jew or Gentile, Mohammedan or Buddhist, atheist or pantheist; he might believe that the world began last year and would end next year, but to believe with the kind of conviction that Reed Smoot possesses that God speaks to him or may speak to him is to admit by the inevitable logic of his conviction that there is a superior authority with whom here and now he may converse, and whose command he can no more refuse to obey than he can will himself not to think.

My brethren and sisters, in my answer to the charges of Mr. Tayler, do you think for a moment that I would admit that I was not to be a Senator because I believed in a living God; because I believed that Joseph Smith was a prophet of the living God, establishing God's work here upon this earth in this dispensation? No. I wanted every Senator and every person in all the world, if it were possible, to understand that the charge that was made against me upon that occasion I agreed was correct as far as my belief in receiving revelations from God, or that Joseph Smith was a prophet of the living God. I never want to live long enough that that testimony shall not be burning in my soul. Rather would I die than have such a thing happen to me. I know that he was a prophet of God. I know that God and his Son Jesus Christ appeared to him. I know that this is the work of God, and just as sure as we live the world will acknowledge it some time or other. (*Reed Smoot*, CR, Oct. 1934, p. 68.)

(2C-5) *More valuable than mortal life.* Let me conclude by saying to you what I have said many times, and what I hope I will ever stand by. I would a thousand times rather go to my grave as I am, with the convictions that I possess, than to falter for one instant in that which God has revealed to me. It is more than mortal life to me. (*Joseph F. Smith*, CR, Apr. 1912, p. 137.)

(2C-6) *Worth more than any sign or gift.* This testimony comes from God; it convinces all to whom it is given in spite of themselves, and it is worth more to men than any sign or gift, because it gives peace, happiness, and contentment to the soul. It assures me that God lives; and if I am faithful, I shall obtain the blessings of the celestial kingdom. (*Joseph Fielding Smith*, CR, Oct. 1968, p. 125.)

(2C-7) *The most useful possession in life.* The most precious thing in all the world is to accept God as our Father, to accept His Son as our Redeemer, our Savior, and to know in one's heart that the Father and the Son appeared in this dispensation and gave the Gospel of Jesus Christ for the happiness, salvation, and exaltation of the human family. To accept that as an eternal truth is to have the greatest possession that the human mind can possess.

I believe with the great English philosopher and scientist, Sir Humphrey Davy, that

If I could choose what of all things would be at the same time the most delightful and the most useful to me, I should prefer a firm religious belief above every other blessing; for this makes life a discipline of goodness; creates new hopes when all earthly ones vanish; throws over the decay of existence the most glorious of all lights; awakens life even in death; makes every torture and shame the ladder of ascent to paradise; and far above all combinations of earthly hopes, calls up the most delightful visions of the future, the security of everlasting joys. . . .

That is the message we should like to give to all the world: that the most delightful, the most useful possession in life is a testimony of the truth of The Church of Jesus Christ of Latter-day Saints. (*David O. McKay*, IN, Apr. 1964, p. 129.)

(2C-8) *Greater than anything else achievable in life.* I would rather have my children and my grandchildren enjoy the companionship of the Holy Ghost, a witness of the divinity of this work, than anything else that they can achieve in this life, or any companionship that they can gain. (*LeGrand Richards*, BYU, 1972-73, p. 40.)

3

REQUIREMENTS FOR OBTAINING A TESTIMONY

A.   A Testimony Comes Only with Effort

(3A-1) *It is obtained by intense strivings.* We can have positive certainty of the reality of a personal God; the continued active life of the Christ, separate from but like his Father; the divinity of the restoration through Joseph Smith and other prophets of the organization and doctrines of God's church on earth; and the power of the divine, authoritative priesthood given to men through revelations from God. These can be known by every responsible person as surely as the knowledge that the sun shines. To fail to attain this knowledge is to admit that one has not paid the price. Like academic degrees, it is obtained by intense strivings. That soul who is clean through repentance and the ordinances receives it if he desires and reaches for it, investigates conscientiously, studies, and prays faithfully. (*Spencer W. Kimball,* FPM, pp. 13-14.)

(3A-2) *The Lord intended that we should work.* Admittedly, it is easier to talk about a testimony than to obtain one. The Lord intended that we should work hard to obtain a testimony, for that will make our testimonies stronger, and they will be more apt to remain with us. Always remember that no good thing comes without effort and sacrifice. When we are required to work for these blessings, we gain knowledge, we develop our skills and our characters, and we learn to overcome evil —

all of which are significant parts of our purpose in life. (O. *Leslie Stone,* CR, Apr. 1975, p. 10.)

(3A-3) *It comes only after you have "hungered and thirsted" for it.* Like the people in the world, you, the youth of the Church, must put forth a similar effort to receive a witness from the Holy Ghost of the reality of the restoration of the gospel. For you, a testimony is not an automatic process; it comes only after you have "hungered and thirsted" for it. This means you must have a desire much more intense than just a passive wanting. (*John H. Vandenberg,* IE, Dec. 1968, p. 110.)

(3A-4) *Time and effort are necessary for the task.* An old adage says there is "no excellence without labor," a truth abundantly supported by human experience. No one becomes learned without study. It has long been admitted that there is no "royal road" to learning. The price of scholarship is many years of continuous hard work. Now, every normal-minded person could become more or less scholarly in some one of the many fields of study. There are very few, however, who do become scholars. Why? You know the answer, it is obvious. It is because they do not give the necessary time and rightly directed effort to the task. But would it be reasonable or consistent for these non-scholars to assert there is no such thing as scholarship? Of course not. Further, there are musicians but most of us are not musicians, some lacking musical talent, but the majority probably lacking inclination. But of those who are musically talented none ever becomes a great musician without years of persistent, continuous work. Great performers continue long hours of practice even though their reputations may be international. . . . No athlete becomes outstanding, no mechanic becomes skilled, no physician becomes an expert, no orator becomes great, no lawyer becomes renowned, except by persistent practice and many, many hours of devoted hard work. These illustrations need not be multiplied. With your attention called to the matter you will readily grant that worthwhile human achievement is attained only by talent coupled with suitably directed toil. Activity is the necessary condition for growth. How foolish it would be for me to close my eyes and ears and say there are no musicians because I am not talented to become a musician; that there are no Edisons because I cannot become an inventor; that there are no artists because I do not have the talents and inclinations to become an artist. Does not reason tell us it is equally foolish for a man to declare there is no God simply because he has not discovered him?

Now, he who makes no attempt to see the great planet Neptune will never see Neptune. It is too far away from the earth and too dimly lighted ever to be seen by the unaided human eye. Likewise he who makes no effort to learn of the existence of Deity will, in this life, likely not learn there is a Deity. But his ignorance does not warrant him in declaring there is no God. (*Joseph F. Merrill*, CN, 1 Sept. 1945, p. 10.)

(3A-5) *Study, pray, act – do something about it!* To have a testimony of God and his Son Jesus Christ can bring about the greatest blessing you can attain in this mortal existence. Each blessing is obtained by fulfilling the law upon which that blessing is predicated. The law upon which this blessing is predicated is given extensively throughout the scriptures.

In Matthew we read: "*Ask*, and it shall be given you; *seek* and ye shall find; *knock*, and it shall be opened unto you: For every one that asketh receiveth; and he that seeketh findeth; and to him that knocketh it shall be opened." (Matthew 7:7-8. Italics added.)

... What does it mean to knock or seek? This is a way of saying, "It requires effort on your part." Study, pray, act — do something about it! Knowledge alone saves no one. Lucifer knows, and it is this knowledge which is to his damnation. Without proper action, it can be the same to anyone else. (*Eldred G. Smith*, CR, Oct. 1964, pp. 9-10.)

(3A-6) *May you not be content with just one experiment.* There is spiritual learning just as there is material learning, and the one without the other is not complete; yet, speaking for myself, if I could have only one sort of learning, that which I would take would be the learning of the spirit, because in the hereafter I shall have opportunity in the eternities which are to come to get the other, and without spiritual learning here my handicaps in the hereafter would be all but overwhelming.

But the Lord has so made it today that we and our children may have both, and that is one of the great glories and blessings which we have today, that we may be learned in the sciences and the arts, and we may also be learned in the spirit. In other words, we may have true knowledge.

Answering the Pharisees, the Lord said: "If any man will do his will, he shall know of the doctrine, whether it be of God, or whether I speak of myself."

I call to the attention of the young people of the Church that this truth of the Master is the challenge of science — the challenge of experimentation. The Lord does not ask us to take his truths without trial. He asks us to test them. Just as a great scientist may announce a great discovery and just as that discovery must be proved, or disproved, by related experiments by the discoverer and by others before it may be wisely accepted or rejected, so the Son of God invites us to test his truths. So I plead with my young brethren and sisters to test the principles of the gospel. Do not throw them over until you have tried them. No chemist ever is satisfied with one experiment, even though it gives an affirmative result. Certainly he is never satisfied with one experiment if it gives a negative result.

So to the youth of Zion I say, Try the Lord, experiment with his principles, nor may you be content with one experiment, particularly if it does not give an affirmative result. And just as a scientific experiment must be performed under proper conditions of heat and light and pressure and absolute cleanliness, so the spiritual experiment must be performed with a pure heart, with a desire to know the truth, with a clean body and a clean mind, in order that the one experimenting may not shut himself off from the very things he desires to know. (*J. Reuben Clark, Jr.*, CR, Apr. 1934, pp. 94-95.)

(3A-7) An *all-out effort is required.* One must be baptized and receive the Holy Ghost and still live the commandments to be given the knowledge of the divinity of the work. Mere passive acceptance of the doctrines will not give the testimony; no casual half-compliance with the program will bring that assurance; but an all-out effort to live his command-ments. We often see this in the lives of members of the Church. One said to me in a recent stake I visited, "I assiduously avoid all testimony meetings. I can't take the sentimental and emotional statements that some of the people make. I can't accept these doctrines unless I can in a cold-blooded and rational way prove every step." I knew this type of man as I have met others like him. In no case had they gone all-out to live the commandments: Little or no tithing, only occasional atten-dance at meetings, considerable criticism of the doctrines, the organi-zations and the leaders, and we know well why they could have no testimony. Remember that the Lord said: "I, the Lord am bound when ye do what I say; but when ye do not what I say; ye have no promise." (Doctrine and Covenants 82:10.) Such people have failed to "do what he says." Of course, they have no promise.

On the other hand we have the missionary completely immersed in his work, giving to it his every thought and energy, and living closely the commandments. Almost without exception they have lived worthily, kept the commandments, and have been rewarded with a knowledge as promised by their Savior, in proportion to their faithfulness. Consider also the thousands of ward, quorum, and stake and mission leaders who have an abiding testimony. It is not blind loyalty but faithful observance, and turning of keys which open the storehouse of spiritual knowledge. (*Spencer W. Kimball*, CR, Oct. 1944, pp. 42-43.)

B.   Following Prescribed Procedures

(3B-1) *You must place yourself in a proper frame of mind.* Now, it is a good question which has been asked by millions since Joseph Smith phrased it: How am I to know which of all, if any, of the organizations is authentic, divine, and recognized by the Lord?

He has given the key. You may *know*. You need not be in doubt. Follow the prescribed procedures, and you may have an absolute knowledge that these things are absolute truths. The necessary procedure is: study, think, pray, and do. Revelation is the key. God will make it known to you once you have capitulated and have become humble and receptive. Having dropped all pride of your mental stature, having acknowledged before God your confusion, having subjected your egotism, and having surrendered yourself to the teaching of the Holy Spirit, you are ready to begin to learn. With preconceived religious notions stubbornly held, one is not teachable. The Lord has promised repeatedly that he will give you a knowledge of spiritual things when you have placed yourself in a proper frame of mind. He has counseled us to seek, ask, and search diligently. These innumerable promises are epitomized by Moroni in the following: "And by the power of the Holy Ghost ye may know the truth of all things." (Moroni 10:5.) What a promise! How extravagant! How wonderful! (*Spencer W. Kimball*, BYU, 1977, p. 142.)

(3B-2) *Important steps in gaining a testimony.* Now, to . . . all . . . who may be sincerely seeking for truth, may I illustrate how they, like a young missionary I met in Chicago, may gain this certainty of knowledge for which all should strive.

This young missionary met me at the train and sought an interview because of his failure during the first few months of his mission to get a testimony of the truth of that which he was teaching.

His attention was called to what the Apostle Paul had said that "your body is the temple of the Holy Ghost which is in you," and that "if any man defile the temple of God, him shall God destroy." The first essential, therefore, in gaining a testimony, is to make certain that one's personal spiritual "house-keeping" is in proper order. His mind and body must be clean if he would enjoy the in-dwelling gift of the Holy Ghost by which he could know the certainty of spiritual things.

The Master took His hearers to one more important step in gaining a testimony when, in answer to the question as to how they were to know whether or not His was true doctrine, He said: "If any man will do his will he shall know of the doctrine, whether it be of God or whether I speak of myself." Thus if you would seek a blessing you must keep the commandments upon which the blessings you seek are predicated.

We concluded our conversation as I pointed out to our young missionary the final, necessary step to gain sure knowledge. The Lord revealed that way to John when he said: "Behold, I stand at the door, and knock: if any man hear my voice, and open the door, I will come in to him, and will sup with him and he with me." (Revelation 3:20.)

When we qualify by righteous living, we place ourselves in tune with the infinite or as Peter puts it, we become "partakers of the divine nature having escaped the corruption that is in the world through lust."

In this condition, the sincere prayer of the righteous heart opens to any individual the door to divine wisdom and strength in that for which he righteously seeks. . . .

A short while ago I was at the stake conference where my young missionary companion of the Chicago railroad incident was called to report his mission. He related the conversation as I have sketched it, and, then declared to the congregation that as a result of his obedience to the counsel he had been given, there came to him an experience which, to use his own words, "that really humbled me and triggered a witness of the Spirit. I felt a quiet excitement within myself that bore witness to certain parts of the Gospel which I had questioned. This feeling grew within me until now I can say that I know this is the true Church of Jesus Christ, that Joseph Smith is a prophet of God, and that the Holy Ghost does live and bear witness of the truth."

As that young missionary came to know, so may everyone who prepares himself, as I have explained, come to know with a certainty which defies all doubt. (*Harold B. Lee*, CN, 14 Jan. 1961, pp. 14-15.)

(3B-3) *Specifically, what must a person do?* A conviction of the truth of the gospel, a testimony, must be sought if it is to be found. It does not come as the dew from heaven. It is the result of man's eagerness to know truth. Often it requires battle with traditions, former opinions and appetites, and a long testing of the gospel by every available fact and standard. "Faith is a gift of God," but faith must be used to be of service to man. The Lord lets it rain upon the just and the unjust, but he whose field is well plowed is most benefited by the moisture from the sky.

Specifically, what must a person do in his quest for a testimony?

First, there must be a desire for truth. That is the beginning of all human progress, in school, in active life, in every human occupation. The desire to know the truth of the gospel must be insistent, constant, overwhelming, burning. It must be a driving force. A "devil-may-care" attitude will not do. Otherwise, the seeker will not pay the required price for the testimony.

A testimony comes only to those who desire it. . . . Desire must precede all else in the winning of a testimony.

Second, the seeker for a testimony must recognize his own limitations. He is on a royal road, traveling towards the palace of truth, in which all human good may be found. There are truths beyond the material universe. Indeed, a testimony may be said to begin with the acceptance of God, who transcends as well as encompasses material things. The seeker for a testimony feels the need of help beyond his own powers, as the astronomer uses the telescope to enlarge his natural vision. The seeker for a testimony prays to the Lord for help. Such a prayer must be as insistent and constant as the desire. They must move together as the palm and back of the hand. Then help will come. Many a man has strayed from the road because his desire has not been coupled with prayer.

Prayer must accompany desire in the quest for a testimony.

Third, an effort must be put forth to learn the gospel, to understand it, to comprehend the relationship of its principles. The gospel must be studied, otherwise no test of its truth may sanely be applied to it. That study must be wide, for the gospel is so organized that in it is a place for every truth, of every name and nature. That study must be constantly continued, for the content of the gospel is illimitable.

It is a paradox that men will gladly devote time every day for many years to learn a science or an art; yet will expect to win a knowledge of the gospel, which comprehends all sciences and arts, through per- functory glances at books or occasional listening to sermons. The gospel should be studied more intensively than any school or college subject. They who pass opinion on the gospel without having given it intimate and careful study are not lovers of truth, and their opinions are worth- less.

To secure a testimony, then, study must accompany desire and prayer.

Fourth, the gospel must be woven into the pattern of life. It must be tested in practice. The gospel must be used in life. That is the ultimate test in the winning of a testimony.

Certainly, the experience of others who have consistently obeyed gospel requirements is of value to the seeker after a testimony. Children are wise in accepting the experiences of their parents. Beginners do well to trust those who are seasoned in gospel living. But, there comes a time when every person must find out for himself, in his own daily life, the value of the gospel. A sufficient testimony comes only to him who "stands upon his own feet."

A testimony of the truth of the gospel comes, then, from: (1) Desire, (2) Prayer, (3) Study, and (4) Practice. (John A. Widtsoe, ER, pp. 15-17.)

(3B-4) *They must be able to bend in humility.* For many years, now, the missionaries have knocked on the doors of the homes of the people of this great city. Most have rejected them, but here and there one or two have accepted the gospel. Why do so many turn their backs on that which is offered or turn away when they have received it? It is because they attempt to understand the words of God by the learning of men. They do not realize that the wisdom of men is as foolishness with God. (See 2 Nephi 9:28.) The Lord has declared that the things of God are understood by the Spirit of God. There must be humility. I want you to think of the bamboo, which stands straight and tall and beautiful, but which can bend to the earth without breaking. So it must be with those who would learn of the things of God. They must be able to bend in humility, to receive the things of the spirit, and having done so, they will rise again to tall and true statures. There must be desire. There must be study of the sacred things of the Lord. There must be prayer, a request to the God of heaven for light and knowledge and understanding. (*Gordon B. Hinckley*, ACR, Aug. 1975 — Hong Kong, pp. 3-4.)

(3B-5) *Prerequisites for a testimony.* All blessings from God come as a result of obedience to the laws upon which they are predicated. This rule, or law, applies to the acquisition of a testimony of the gospel or any related subject. Any accountable person can gain a testimony if he will obey the laws upon which the receipt of such knowledge is predicated. But here, as elsewhere, there are certain prerequisites, which may be listed roughly as follows:

1. The seeker must desire to know the truth of the gospel or whatever is involved in his quest.

2. He must study and learn everything possible with relation to the matter involved. In John 5:39 we read: "Search the scriptures; for in them ye think ye have eternal life." And we are directed in the Doctrine and Covenants 1:37 to "Search these commandments."

3. The applicant must practice the principles and truths which he learns and bring his life into harmony with them. The Savior said: "My doctrine is not mine, but his that sent me. If any man will do his will, he shall know of the doctrine, whether it be of God, or whether I speak of myself." (John 7:16-17.)

4. He must constantly pray to the Father and exercise faith that the truth will be manifested by revelation through the Holy Ghost. (*Hugh B. Brown*, RS, Oct. 1969, pp. 724-725.)

(3B-6) *Three rules for acquisition of spiritual knowledge.* The acquisition of understanding and enthusiasm for the Lord comes from following simple rules, and in conclusion, I should like to suggest three, elementary in their concept, almost trite in their repetition, but fundamental in their application and fruitful in their result. I suggest them particularly to our young people.

The first is to read — to read the word of the Lord. I know that with the demands of your studies there is little time to read anything else. But I promise you that if you will read the words of that writing which we call scripture, there will come into your heart an understanding and a warmth that will be pleasing to experience. "Search the scriptures; for in them ye think ye have eternal life: and they are they which testify of me." (John 5:39.) Read, for instance, the Gospel of John from its beginning to its end. Let the Lord speak for himself to you, and his words will come with a quiet conviction that will make the words of his critics meaningless. Read also the testament of the New World, the Book of Mormon, brought forth as a witness "that Jesus is the Christ, the Eternal God, manifesting himself unto all nations." (Book of Mormon title page.)

The next is to serve — to serve in the work of the Lord. Spiritual strength is like physical strength; it is like the muscle of my arm. It grows only as it is nourished and exercised.

The cause of Christ does not need your doubts; it needs your strength and time and talents; and as you exercise these in service, your faith will grow and your doubts will wane.

The Lord declared: "He that findeth his life shall lose it: and he that loseth his life for my sake shall find it." (Matthew 10:39.)

These words have something more than a cold theological meaning. They are a statement of a law of life — that as we lose ourselves in a great cause we find ourselves — and there is no greater cause than that of the Master.

The third is to pray. Speak with your Eternal Father in the name of his Beloved Son. "Behold," he says, "I stand at the door, and knock; if any man hear my voice, and open the door, I will come in to him, and will sup with him, and he with me." (Revelation 3:20.)

This is his invitation, and the promise is sure. It is unlikely that you will hear voices from heaven, but there will come a heaven-sent assurance, peaceful and certain.

In that great conversation between Jesus and Nicodemus, the Lord declared: "That which is born of the flesh is flesh; and that which is born of the Spirit is spirit." Then he went on to say, "The wind bloweth where it listeth, and thou hearest the sound thereof, but canst not tell whence it cometh, and whither it goeth: so is every one that is born of the Spirit." (John 3:6, 8.)

I do not hesitate to promise that so it will be with you. If you will read the word of the Lord, if you will serve in his cause, if in prayer you will talk with him, your doubts will leave; and shining through all of the confusion of philosophy, so-called higher criticism, and negative theology will come the witness of the Holy Spirit that Jesus is in very deed the Son of God, born in the flesh, the Redeemer of the world resurrected from the grave, the Lord who shall come to reign as King of kings. It is your opportunity so to know. It is your obligation so to find out. (*Gordon B. Hinckley*, CR, Apr. 1966, pp. 86-87.)

(3B-7) *Wrapping ourselves in obedience.* I know some people who will say, "Well, how can I conduct my life so as to be responsive to the message that comes from an unseen world?" There is an old illustration — a high school illustration — that bears on this subject: We may take a rod of soft iron and place it with some filings without apparently causing any change — the rod is not magnetic. But if we wrap the rod with a wire carrying an electric current, it becomes a magnet. Though the rod has not changed in shape and width and length, it has undergone a deep change. It has become changed so that it attracts iron filings or whatever else is subject to magnetic action. Just so, if we — men and women — could wrap ourselves in obedience to God's love, and live as we should, a wonderful change is effected in us, and we too can then hear the messages from the unseen world. (*Harold B. Lee*, BYU, 15 Oct. 1952, p. 4.)

(3B-8) *The foundation for the search.* Two conditions precede the actual building of a testimony. First, there must be an earnest desire for certain knowledge of truth. This desire must be of such a nature that when truth is found, it is accepted, though it may run counter to previous teachings and traditions. Second, help in the search must be sought in prayer from the unseen world, from the Lord. When these two conditions are complied with, the doors to a testimony will be thrown wide open.

Upon such a foundation the search for a testimony begins with a study of the gospel.

One must know the principles of the gospel to bear proper witness of their truth. It is not necessary to know all, but as far as a person's knowledge goes, he can bear testimony of its truth. It is so in any pursuit of knowledge. The young chemist may know only a small part of the vast field covered by that science, but to that which he has learned he can testify.

Yet, knowledge by itself is not sufficient. Any person may learn to understand gospel principles from books or teachers, as he may learn any chapter in a textbook. Nevertheless, he may remain an unbeliever. Many a person knows the gospel as taught by the Church, yet remains outside its pale.

The insufficiency of knowledge alone was implied by James the apostle when he said, ". . . the devils also believe, and tremble." (James 2:19.) Certainly they know, for they were present in the great pre-existent council when the plan of salvation was unfolded by the Father. They knew then its metes and bounds, but refused to try it out. With their barren knowledge they tremble for fear of their own futures.

Whatever has been learned must be tried out, used in the process of living. Then we shall know of its truth. Knowledge of the gospel must be incorporated into one's life, else the testimony sounds hollow and is without life. Only when knowledge is used, can we win a full conviction, a certainty, of the truth of the gospel, and a full comprehension of it.

In short, knowing and doing lead to the revelation from God which we call a testimony. Neither can do it alone. This was the great message of James the apostle, ". . . faith, if it hath not works, is dead, being alone." (James 2:17.) (John A. Widtsoe, IE, May 1945, p. 273.)

(3B-9) *Introducing it into your very being.* But how may we *know* him? That is the next question. Has he at any time, or on any occasion, answered that question? If so, we want the answer, because it is vital. In searching the record as it is given to us by men who associated daily with the Lord, we find that upon one occasion men who were listening to him cried out against him. They opposed his works, as men today oppose him. And one voice cried out and said in effect, "How do we know that what you tell us is true? How do we know that your profession of being the Son of God is true?" And Jesus answered him in just a simple way (and note the test): *"If any man will do his will, he shall know of the doctrine, whether it be of God, or whether I speak of myself."* (John 7:17. Italics added.)

The test is most sound. It is most philosophical. It is the most simple test to give knowledge to an individual of which the human mind can conceive. *Doing* a thing, *introducing it into your very being,* will convince you whether it is good or whether it is bad. You may not be able to convince me of that which you know, but *you know it because you have lived it.* That is the test that the Savior gave to those men when they asked him how they should know whether the doctrine was of God or whether it was of man. (*David O. McKay,* CR, Oct. 1966, p. 136.)

(3B-10) *How does one receive a message from the Holy Ghost?* Moroni said: "... by the power of the Holy Ghost ye may know the truth of all things." (Moroni 10:5.) One may ask, "How does one receive a message from the Holy Ghost?" ...

Now, I think if we will apply some of the laws of electronics, that is, radio and television, we will be aided in a possible understanding of how we can receive a message from the Holy Ghost. We have a spirit mind and a mortal mind. Our spirit mind can receive messages from the Holy Ghost, who is a spirit.

In this room now there are many waves going by of sound, of pictures, and even of colored pictures. We cannot detect them with our mortal eyes or ears, but if we set up a receiving set and put it in tune, then we pick up the sound or pictures by the mortal ears or eyes. Similarly, the Holy Ghost may be constantly sending out messages like a broadcasting station. If you put yourself in tune, that is, knock or ask or seek, you may receive the message. It may be as if you were to open an imaginary window or door between your spirit mind and your physical mind and permit the message to come through. Spirit can talk to spirit, and you are part spirit — just open that imaginary door and let the mortal mind receive. To open it requires study, prayer, action or works, or knock, and it shall be opened unto you. (*Eldred G. Smith,* CR, Oct. 1964, pp. 10-11.)

(3B-11) *That one experience was worth more than all the theories that men have produced.* When you go to school, you study mathematics or chemistry or some foreign language. You do not just take the teacher's word for what is given there. When you study mathematics, you actually work out the equations and know by working them out that they are true. And when you study chemistry, you learn about the truths of that subject by actually performing the experiments that are given to you, and by performing them you discover the truth of the principles you are taught.

But if you went to school all your life and did not study mathematics, you would never know anything about that subject, would you? You might go to school all your life and never learn one thing about chemistry, unless you studied chemistry. And you can be in this Church all your life, and never know what this Church teaches unless you study it. . . .

Open the pages of the Bible; read there of the hand dealings of God to man. Read there of the life of the Savior. Learn of his teachings. He actually was here on the earth, and he taught men the principles about which you have heard today and in the preceding days of this conference.

And read the Book of Mormon. Study its pages. Know what is inside the covers of that great book. And will you study also the revelations that are given in that very small but great book, The Pearl of Great Price? It is almost unknown among many people, and yet it contains some of the greatest revelations of God to man.

And then, young people, will you really make a study of the life of the Prophet Joseph Smith and read the revelations that God gave to him? Discover Joseph Smith. Find out what motivated him. Be thrilled with the rest of us as you read the story of his going into the woods and there kneeling down and asking for light; and in response to that prayer seeing the Father and the Son standing there before him, not in some dream, but in a real experience.

And then read of his visits with the Angel Moroni, a personage who came back from the dead and ministered to Joseph Smith, gave him direction, and helped him in the production of the Book of Mormon. And then read the story of Oliver Cowdery and Joseph Smith who received ministrations from John the Baptist, and the Apostles, Peter, James and John.

Read the story of these two men as they knelt in the Kirtland Temple in prayer, and there suddenly came before them a glorious vision. In the Kirtland Temple, here in the United States of America, stood the Savior, the Redeemer of the world. They saw him and talked with him. That one experience was worth more than all the philosophies and scientific theories that men have produced in all time. They saw him; they heard his voice; they knew that he lived; and they did not have to take anybody else's ideas or hypotheses pertaining to it.

After his appearance there came other glorious personages, Elijah,

Moses, Elias. Why, this Dispensation of the Fulness of Times is so filled with actual experiences which men have had with God, and with the testimonies of those men, that you do not need to doubt. You may know for yourself as well, because as you study these things, and as you work in the Church, if you will pray, . . . then the Lord will bless you with a knowledge of the truth of these things. You will receive a testimony, and you will know for yourself that God does live, that Mormonism is true, that the Savior has a modern ministry, and that we are part of it. (*Mark E. Petersen*, CR, Apr. 1952, pp. 106-107.)

(3B-12) *How a knowledge of the truth is obtained.* In my judgment one of the first cornerstones of all righteousness in this world is for a person to get for himself a knowledge, by the revelations of the Holy Ghost to his soul, that this work in which we are engaged is true. How does one get such a knowledge? God is no respecter of persons and he, through the Holy Ghost, will reveal to every person who abides the law upon which the receipt of that revelation is predicated, a knowledge that this work is true. The first step in complying with that law is for a person to desire to know. Men are given according to their desires, and unless they desire in their hearts to know that this work is true, that Jesus is the Christ and that Joseph Smith was a Prophet of God, they will never exert the effort, and they will never comply with the law which will entitle them to know. And I think that the second step is that they must study the principles of the kingdom. The Lord does not pour a testimony into a vacuum. Men have to know what the doctrines of the kingdom are. Men are saved no faster than they gain knowledge of Jesus Christ and the principles of salvation. No man can be saved in ignorance of Jesus Christ and the laws of salvation. Christ said to the Jews: "Search the scriptures; for in them ye think ye have eternal life: and they are they which testify of me." (John 5:39.)

He said in our day as the preface to his Book of Commandments: "Search these commandments, for they are true and faithful, and the prophecies and promises which are in them shall all be fulfilled."

We have to learn of the doctrines of the kingdom if we ever in this world expect to gain a revelation that those doctrines are true.

And the third step is that we must practice the principles which we learn. The Lord said: " . . . My doctrine is not mine, but his that sent me. If any man will do his will, he shall know of the doctrine, whether it be of God, or whether I speak of myself." (John 7:16-17.)

We must practice the principles which we learn and make them a living part of our lives.

And as a fourth step, because a testimony comes by the revelations of the Holy Ghost and not from any other source, we must pray to the Lord in humility and in faith and beseech him to reveal to us whether this work is true or whether it is not. In writing of the things that were on the gold plates, Moroni said this: "And when ye shall receive these things, I would exhort you that ye would ask God the eternal Father, in the name of Christ, if these things are not true; and if ye shall ask with a sincere heart, with real intent, having faith in Christ, he will manifest the truth of it unto you, by the power of the Holy Ghost. And by the power of the Holy Ghost ye may know the truth of all things." (Moroni 10:4-5.)

Now there is not a person, a God-fearing and righteous person in this world, who cannot come to this kingdom and by obedience to that law, embracing those four steps, gain for himself a knowledge that this work is true, a knowledge that Jesus is the Christ, that Joseph Smith was the head of this dispensation and that the keys of the kingdom are with the Saints today. (*Bruce R. McConkie*, CR, Apr. 1947, pp. 39-40.)

(3B-13) *And yet the spirit of God will not burn in their hearts.* I have met many young men who have said to me, "I do not know that the Gospel is true. I believe it, but I do not know it." I have invariably replied to them that our Lord and Master has said that he who will do the will of the Father shall know of the doctrine, whether it be of God, or whether he spoke of himself, and if they would do the will of the Father, they should eventually have a knowledge of the Gospel. Some of them have said: "Oh, if I could only see an angel; if I could only hear speaking in tongues; if I could only see some great manifestation, then I would believe." I wish to say to all within the sound of my voice that the seeing of angels and great manifestations do not make great men in the Church and kingdom of God. Think of the three witnesses to the Book of Mormon. What is their testimony? It is that an angel showed them the plates, and that they knew they had been translated by the gift and power of God. . . . Yet these men fell by the wayside, though they remained true and steadfast to their testimony of the Book of Mormon.

. . . So it has been in all ages of the world, and so it will be with those who do not keep the commandments of God. Angels may visit them, they may see visions, they may have dreams, they may even see the Son of God, and yet the Spirit of God will not burn in their hearts. But those who do the will of God, and live God-like lives, they will grow and increase in the testimony of the Gospel and in power and ability to do God's will. (*Heber J. Grant,* CR, Apr. 1900, pp. 22-23.)

(3B-14) *This formula when followed will bring a conviction.* I have borne my testimony many times to people who were interested in knowing more about the Church, and they have asked me: "How can I obtain a conviction of the truthfulness of the restored gospel — yes, a testimony to this effect?" My answer has been, "Study the gospel, pray and attend church."

This formula when followed will bring a conviction or testimony that the restored gospel of Jesus Christ is true, and when one accepts the gospel plan and lives its principles, it will bring him peace, happiness, growth, and development. However, to obtain a testimony one must have a real desire to know the truth and must be willing to exert considerable effort.

The interested person must study the gospel, and the gospel is to be found primarily in the Bible, Book of Mormon, Doctrine and Covenants, and Pearl of Great Price, the four standard works of The Church of Jesus Christ of Latter-day Saints. . . .

Through study of the scriptures we can understand our relationship to God and how the basic gospel principles apply to our daily lives. Our study, however, should be constant and intensive, for the gospel of Jesus Christ embraces all truth.

Now regarding the second step to acquire a testimony — prayer — the Prophet Joseph Smith observed that "it is the first principle of the gospel to know for a certainty the character of God, and to know that we may converse with Him as one man converses with another. . . ." (*Documentary History of the Church,* vol. 6, p. 305.)

Near the end of the Book of Mormon, Moroni, a great leader, gave this promise: "And when ye shall receive these things, I would exhort you that ye would ask God, the Eternal Father, in the name of Christ, if these things are not true; and if ye shall ask with a sincere heart, with real intent, having faith in Christ, he will manifest the truth of it unto you, by the power of the Holy Ghost. And by the power of the Holy Ghost ye may know the truth of all things." (Moroni 10:4-5.)

Although this promise specifically refers to the Book of Mormon, I am sure as you study the Bible, the Doctrine and Covenants, and the

Pearl of Great Price you will find that the promise is likewise applicable to these scriptures. . . .

Prayer then must accompany study for one to obtain a testimony of the truthfulness of the restored gospel.

The third part of the formula to obtain a testimony is to attend church and become involved in church activities. . . .

Many thousands have received a testimony, a conviction of the truthfulness of the restored gospel, by following the formula: study, pray, and attend church. They have thus been able to better interpret the scriptures and find their place in the eternal scheme of things. (*Franklin D. Richards*, CR, Apr. 1974, pp. 84-86.)

(3B-15) *The way to obtain a testimony is clear.* To those who truly desire a testimony of the truthfulness of the gospel, the way to obtain one is clear. First, the Lord asks that we study the gospel diligently. In speaking to Oliver Cowdery, he made the importance of diligent study very clear: "Behold, you have not understood; you have supposed that I would give it unto you, when you took no thought save it was to ask me. But, behold, I say unto you, that you must study it out in your mind; then you must ask me if it be right. . . . (Doctrine and Covenants 9:7-8.)

As the Lord indicates, diligent study of the gospel is vital in order to gain a testimony. Study of the gospel builds faith; it provides evidence upon which one's testimony can be built. The apostle Paul said that faith is based on "evidence" (Hebrews 11:1), and study will provide that evidence.

Coupled with personal study, a second most important step in obtaining a personal testimony is that you live the gospel and keep the commandments. The Savior spoke regarding this step toward gaining a testimony. He said: "My doctrine is not mine, but his that sent me. If any man will do his will, he shall know of the doctrine, whether it be of God, or whether I speak of myself." (John 7:16-17.)

Alma, the Nephite prophet, made a similar declaration as he challenged the people to experiment upon his words. He said, " . . . behold, if ye will awake and arouse your faculties, even to an experiment upon my words, and exercise a particle of faith, yea, even if ye can no more than desire to believe, let this desire work in you, even until ye believe in a manner that ye can give place for a portion of my words." (Alma 32:27.)

Obedience to the commandments of God is essential if a person is to be prepared to receive a testimony. . . .

Third, to gain a testimony, you must approach the Father in humble prayer, just as did the Prophet Joseph. As Joseph Smith found, and thousands of others confirm, the following declaration of the Lord is true: "If any of you lack wisdom, let him ask of God, that giveth to all men liberally, and upbraideth not; and it shall be given him." (James 1:5.) (*John H. Vandenberg,* IE, Dec. 1968, p. 111.)

(3B-16) *Live by faith first, then knowledge comes.* President John Henry Smith gave this advice: "If you want to have a testimony about any part of it [meaning the gospel] live that part and you will get your testimony. It does not matter what principle it is, live the principle for awhile and get your own testimony." This is very sage advice for all to follow. We must learn to live by faith before the witness of knowledge is received. Christ said to the doubting Thomas: "Blessed are they that have not seen, and yet have believed." (John 20:29.) (*Delbert L. Stapley,* BYU, 23 Mar. 1971, pp. 2-3.)

C. The Necessity of Conforming to Gospel Laws

(3C-1) *Unless it is merited it will not come.* [A testimony] cannot be imposed upon a person nor upon a people. It comes only by a self-disciplined obedience to the laws upon which it is based. Unless it is merited it will not come, regardless of our hopes and good intentions. Each person, with the help of God, must acquire it for himself. (*Marion G. Romney,* CN, 17 July 1943, p. 8.)

(3C-2) *Teach me all that I must do.* As the Savior taught in the temple on one occasion, the Jews marvelled at his wisdom and knowledge. "How knoweth this man letters, having never learned?" they asked. "Jesus answered them, and said, My doctrine is not mine, but his that sent me. If any man will do his will, he shall know of the doctrine, whether it be of God, or whether I speak of myself." (John 7:14-17.) The key phrase, of course, is, "If any man will do his will." The doing is of prime importance.

We are always touched when we hear a chorus of Primary children sing, "I Am a Child of God." The last two lines of that inspired song read: "Teach me all that I must know, To live with Him some day." I understand that future printings will follow a wise suggestion made by Brother Kimball, that the word "know" be changed to "do." "Teach me all that I must *do*, To live with Him some day." Only in the doing can we be assured of a confirmation by the spirit — yes, by good works we do become eligible for personal revelation. (*Robert L. Simpson*, CR, Oct. 1965, p. 78.)

(3C-3) *A three-month experiment.* I am reminded of two young men who came in to see me some months ago. They had been recommended by their priesthood leaders. From the moment they stepped into the office, they began in a very sincere way questioning certain doctrines and teachings and procedures of the Church. Their attitude, however, was not antagonistic, as they were sincerely looking for answers.

I asked them finally if their questions perhaps represented the symptoms of their problem and not the cause. Wasn't their real question whether or not this church is true? Whether or not it is actually the Church of Jesus Christ? And whether or not it is led by divine revelation? The young men agreed that perhaps if they were sure of the answers to these questions, they could take care of the other questions that seemed to arise in their hearts.

I asked them if they were willing to participate in an experiment. One of them appeared to be athletically inclined, and so I turned to him and asked, "If you wanted to learn about the chemical properties of water, would you go to the local sports stadium and run four laps around the track?"

He said, "Of course not."

I asked, "Why not?"

He said, "The two are not related."

We then turned to John, chapter seven, and read: "If any man will do his will, he shall know of the doctrine, whether it be of God, or whether I speak of myself." (John 7:17.)

If we are going to experiment with the things of Christ, then we are going to have to put these things to a spiritual test — a test that the Savior himself has outlined for all those who wish to know, a test of doing.

I asked them if they read the scriptures.

They said, "No."

I asked them if they prayed.

They said, "Not often."

I asked them if they kept the Word of Wisdom.

They said, "Occasionally."

I asked them if they went to church.

They said they'd stopped.

I asked them if they would be interested in a three-month experiment. They said they would try but were not anxious to commit themselves until they found out what I had in mind.

"During the next three months will you attend all your church meetings and listen carefully to what is being said, even taking notes of the principal points being made by the teachers and how these points might apply to your lives?"

They thought for a moment and said they would.

"During the next three months will you reinstitute in your personal life prayer, night and morning, thanking God for the blessings you enjoy and asking him to help you know if the Church is true and if the things you are doing are meaningful to your lives?"

One of these young men, who considered himself an agnostic, balked at this, but then he finally agreed to do it on the basis that for the sake of the experiment he would accept the premise that there is a God and would appeal to this God for the light and knowledge which he was seeking.

I asked them if in the next three months they would refrain from drinking, smoking, and drugs. Although this created some anxiety, they resolved to do it.

I asked them if in the next three months they would resolve to keep themselves morally clean and in harmony with the principles of virtue which the Savior taught. They said they would. And then I suggested they establish a schedule, on their own, during the next three months to read the Book of Mormon from cover to cover — a few pages each day, with a prayer at each reading that the Lord would bless them to know if the book is true and actually from him. They agreed.

Anticipating what might happen, I said, "Now, if you feel disposed to tell your friends about this, probably their first comment will be 'Boy, has Brother Dunn snowed you.' You may even feel that way a time or two during this experiment, but don't let it keep you from doing what you have agreed to do. If you think that might be a problem, then keep it in the back of your mind, and go ahead and honestly experiment, and let this three-month experience speak for itself." I added, "If things go properly, you'll notice some by-products, such as a growing awareness and concern for your fellowman and greater appreciation and consideration for other people." They accepted the challenge and left.

Of course, what was really hoped for was the experience that every member has a right to enjoy and everyone else has the right to receive, and that is the knowledge of a personal testimony. I think Brigham Young described it best when he said:

> There is no other experience known to mortal man that can be compared with the testimony or witness of the Holy Ghost. It is as powerful as a two-edged sword and burns in the breast of man like a consuming fire. It destroys fear and doubt, leaving in their stead absolute unqualified, and incontrovertible knowledge that a principle or thing is true. . . .
>
> This same testimony has sustained faithful saints to the present day and will be a lamp to their path forever. The effect of this testimony reaches above and beyond all physical or earthly things and makes relationship with God the Father a literal, pulsing fact. Every fiber of both body and spirit respond to the witness of that testimony and the soul knows and lives the truth.

(*Loren C. Dunn*, CR, Apr. 1971, pp. 106-107.)

(3C-4) *To those who would give everything they have for a testimony.* I have met any number of people who have said: "Oh, I wish that I had that faith and that knowledge which you claim to have. I would give everything in the world for it."

I remember distinctly that one of my friends said to me: "I would give everything I had in the wide world if I had the knowledge you claim to have, and that your brother, B. F., claims to have."

I laughed and said: "That sounds very fine, but there is only one trouble about it, and that is that there is not a word of truth in it. We do not ask you to give everything you have. We ask only, my dear friend, that you quit swearing when you get mad, that you quit smoking cigars, and that you quit gambling."

He said: "I never was drunk."

"No, you never were drunk, but I have heard you say a lot of things that I know you were not proud of after you were sober. And you have got to quit gambling."

He said: "I wouldn't gamble."

"But you play cards with your friends and take twenty-five to fifty dollars a month away from them as regularly as you draw your salary. In fact, I once heard you say that you generally pay twenty-five or fifty dollars a month on your debts by enjoying yourself playing cards. You are just smart enough that if you did not win you would quit playing. So you are a gambler. Now all you have to do to acquire that which you say you 'would give everything in the world for' is to make of yourself a better father, better husband, a better citizen, and ask the Lord to forgive you for doing the things that he has revealed in our day men ought not to do. And after you get a testimony of the gospel, the same as I have, and the same as my brother Fred has, we do not want all you have got — we want you to keep ninety percent of it, but we may come around and ask you to give us a little of the ninety percent to help build meetinghouses and for other purposes. We do not want it all. You do not have to give all you have got and all you will get; you don't have to give 'everything in the world,' as you say you would — all you have to do is to give away your bad habits, and change your life, make a better individual of yourself, and keep the commandments of God."

I regret that he never did. (*Heber J. Grant,* IE, Sept. 1943, p. 525.)

(3C-5) *Many members have not received because they fail to conform.* It is the duty of each member of the Church to live humbly, sincerely, and in strict obedience to the commandments that have been given. If this is done, a man will know the truth. Evidently there are many members of the Church who have not received a testimony simply because they do not make their lives conform to the requirements of the gospel. The Spirit of the Lord cannot dwell in unclean tabernacles, and because of this the knowledge which is promised is not received. Then again, there are members of the Church who take no time to inform themselves by study and faith, and all such are without the inspiration which the faithful are promised. When this is the case, those who are guilty are easily deceived and are in danger of turning away to false doctrines and theories of men. The Lord has given us the key by which the truth may be known and error detected. Said he: "My doctrine is not mine, but his that sent me. If any man will do his will, he shall know of the doctrine, whether it be of God, or whether I speak of myself." (John 7:16-17.)

Again he said: "If ye continue in my word, then are ye my disciples indeed; And ye shall know the truth, and the truth shall make you free." (John 8:31-32.) (*Joseph Fielding Smith*, IE, June 1959, p. 409.)

(3C-6) *Our manner of life must change.* Nephi was a great prophet of God. He taught his brothers a great truth . . . by referring to what God had said: "If ye will not harden your hearts, and ask me in faith, believing that ye shall receive, with diligence in keeping my commandments, surely these things shall be made known unto you." (1 Nephi 15:11.)

Thus if we follow the directions of God and do as he asks us to do, then pray about it, we will receive not only knowledge, but also blessings that will help us to be happier in our families and to find greater joy in life. The only restriction placed on us is that we live our lives in full conformance to the commandments of God. For even if we ask for light and knowledge, but refuse to change our manner of life, God cannot bless us.

This is the same practice we follow as parents. If I have a disobedient son who refuses to follow my directions, I cannot reward and bless him for his actions. I still love him, but I cannot reward him until he changes his actions and becomes dutiful and obedient. We should remember this in our dealings with God. As we conform our lives to his direction, then he can reward us with greater light and knowledge. (*Theodore M. Burton*, ACR, Aug. 1975 — Seoul, Korea, p. 6.)

(3C-7) *Action is one of the chief foundations of personal testimony.* One of the most dynamic challenges in the scriptures comes at the end of King Benjamin's address to his people as he concludes his ministry and turns the reins of government over to his son, Mosiah. Standing on the tower he built to address the people, he guides them through the fundamentals of the gospel and commits them to the wisdom, power, and purposes of God, making this most important challenge: " . . . and now, if you believe all these things see that ye do them." (Mosiah 4:10.) The sincerity of their belief must be demonstrated in the verity in their actions.

Action is one of the chief foundations of personal testimony. The surest witness is that which comes firsthand out of personal experience.

When the Jews challenged the doctrine Jesus taught in the temple, he answered, " . . . my doctrine is not mine, but his that sent me." Then he added the key to personal testimony, "If any man will do his will, he shall know of the doctrine, whether it be of God, or whether I speak of myself." (John 7:16-17.)

Do we hear the imperative in this declaration of the Savior? "If any man will *do . . .* he will *know!*" John caught the significance of this imperative and emphasized its meaning in his gospel. He said, "He that saith he abideth in him ought himself also so to walk, even as he walked." (1 John 2:6.)

Merely saying, accepting, believing are not enough. They are incomplete until that which they imply is translated into the dynamic action of daily living. This, then, is the finest source of personal testimony. One knows because he has experienced. He does not have to say, "Brother Jones says it is true, and I believe him." He can say, "I have lived this principle in my own life, and I know through personal experience that it works. I have felt its influence, tested its practical usefulness, and know that it is good. I can testify of my own knowledge that it is a true principle." (*Howard W. Hunter*, CR, Apr. 1967, pp. 115-116.)

(3C-8) *Why are some so sure while others are passive?* In a high council testimony meeting some time ago I heard one of the number say: "I am happy in the work and have made research and this Church and its doctrines satisfy me better than anything I have found." Then another arose and with deep feeling declared: "This is the work of God, I *know it.* It is the Lord's eternal plan of exaltation. I *know* that Jesus lives and is the Redeemer." I was uplifted by his sureness. And I went to the revelations of the Lord to see how it is that some are so sure while others are passive or have doubts.

I recall the experience of the Apostles when the Lord manifested himself to them after his resurrection and found a group who accepted him, but one of the quorum being absent declared that he would not believe unless he could see in the Lord's hands the print of the nails, and thrust his hand into the wounded side. And when the Savior, anticipating his doubt, had commanded Thomas to thrust forth his hand and feel and know, he said: " . . . Thomas, because thou hast seen me, thou hast believed: blessed are they that have not seen, and yet have believed." (John 20:29.)

The Lord thus indicated that a knowledge of spiritual things may be had without perception through the five senses. He has keys by which we may have a knowledge of his work. In the temple he taught the Jews. They marvelled at his knowledge and positiveness and said: "He speaks as one having authority."

The Redeemer declared: " . . . My doctrine is not mine, but his that sent me. If any man will do his will, he will know of the doctrine, whether it be of God or whether I speak of myself." (John 7:16-17.)

What is it to *know* of the doctrine? It is an unwavering assurance. The Lord has offered a rich reward but has provided that it can be had only by meeting certain requirements. He has said: "There is a law, irrevocably decreed in heaven before the foundations of this world, upon which all blessings are predicated — and when we obtain any blessing from God, it is by obedience to that law upon which it is predicated." (Doctrine and Covenants 130:20-21.)

In this case the blessing promised is a *knowledge of the divinity of the doctrine.* And in this case the law or requirement is that one must "do his will." Most of us know what his will is, far more than we have disposition or ability to comply.

The Lord has reiterated his promise with much emphasis: "If thou shalt ask, thou shalt receive revelation upon revelation, knowledge upon knowledge, that thou mayest know the mysteries and peaceable things — that which bringeth joy, that which bringeth life eternal." (Doctrine and Covenants 42:61.) (*Spencer W. Kimball,* CR, Oct. 1944, pp. 41-42.)

(3C-9) *Worthiness is essential to receive direction and guidance.* We had a very grievous case that had to come before the high council and the stake presidency, which resulted in the excommunication of a man of a family who had harmed a lovely young girl. After nearly an all-night session which resulted in that action, I went to my office rather weary the next morning, to be confronted by a brother of this man whom we had had on trial the night before. This man said, "I want to tell you that my brother wasn't guilty of that thing which you charged him with."

"How do you know he wasn't guilty?" I asked.

"Because I prayed, and the Lord told me he was innocent," the man answered.

I asked him to come into the office and we sat down, and I asked, "Would you mind if I asked you a few personal questions?"

He said, "Certainly not."

"How old are you?"

"Forty-seven."

"What priesthood do you hold?"

He said he thought he was a teacher.

"Do you keep the Word of Wisdom?"

He said, "Well, no." He used tobacco, which was obvious.

"Do you pay your tithing?"

He said, "No" — and he didn't intend to as long as that blankety-blank-blank man was the bishop of the Thirty-Second Ward.

I said, "Do you attend your priesthood meetings?"

He replied, "No, sir!" and he didn't intend to as long as that man was bishop.

"You don't attend your sacrament meetings either?"

"No, sir."

"Do you have your family prayers?"

He said, "No."

"Do you study the scriptures?"

He said, well, his eyes were bad and he couldn't read very much.

I then said to him: "In my home I have a beautiful instrument called a radio. When everything is in good working order we can dial it to a certain station and pick up a speaker or the voice of a singer all the way across the continent. . . . But, after we have used it for a long time, there are some little delicate instruments . . . on the inside called radio tubes that begin to wear out. . . . If we don't give that attention . . . the radio sits there looking quite like it did before, but something has happened on the inside. We can't get any singer. We can't get any speaker.

"Now," I said, "you and I have within our souls something like . . . a counterpart of those radio tubes. We might have what we call a 'Go-to-Sacrament Meeting' tube, 'Keep-the-Word-of-Wisdom' tube, 'Pay-Your-Tithing' tube, 'Have-Your-Family-Prayers' tube, 'Read-the-Scriptures' tube, and, as one of the most important, that might be said to be the master tube of our whole soul, the 'Keep-Yourselves-Morally-Clean' tube. If one of these becomes worn out by disuse or is not active — we fail to keep the commandments of God — it has the same effect upon our spiritual selves that that same worn-out instrument in the radio in my home has upon the reception that we otherwise could receive from a distance.

"Now, then," I said, "fifteen of the best living men in the Pioneer Stake prayed last night. They heard the evidence, and every man was united in saying that your brother was guilty. Now, you, who do none of these things, you say you prayed, and you got an opposite answer. How would you explain that?"

Then this man gave an answer that I think was a classic. He said, "Well, President Lee, I think I must have gotten my answer from the wrong source." And you know that is just as great a truth as we can have. We get our answer from the source of the power we list to obey. If we are keeping the commandments of the Devil, we will get the answer from the Devil. If we are keeping the commandments of God, we will get the commandments from our Heavenly Father for our direction and for our guidance. (*Harold B. Lee*, BYU, 15 Oct. 1952, pp. 4-6.)

(3C-10) *The Holy Ghost will not dwell with the disobedient.* Now I am going to say something that maybe I could not prove, but I believe it is true, that we have a great many members of this Church who have never received a manifestation through the Holy Ghost. Why? Because they have not made their lives conform to the truth. And the Holy Ghost will not dwell in unclean tabernacles or disobedient tabernacles. The Holy Ghost will not dwell with that person who is unwilling to obey and keep the commandments of God or who violates those commandments willfully. In such a soul the spirit of the Holy Ghost cannot enter. That great gift comes to us only through humility and faith and obedience. Therefore, a great many members of the Church do not have that guidance. Then some cunning, crafty individual will come along teaching that which is not true, and without the guidance which is promised to us through our faithfulness, people are unable to discern and are led astray. It depends on our faithfulness and our obedience to the commandments of the Lord if we have the teachings, the enlightening instruction, that comes from the Holy Ghost.

When we are disobedient, when our minds are set upon the things of this world rather than on the things of the kingdom of God, we cannot have the manifestations of the Holy Ghost. Did you ever stop to think what a great privilege it is for us to have the companionship of one of the members of the Godhead? Have you thought of it that way? That is our privilege, if we keep the commandments the Lord has given us. (*Joseph Fielding Smith*, BYU, 25 Oct. 1961, pp. 4-5.)

(3C-11) *They must test the principles.* They who want to know the truth of the latter-day message must try to live according to its requirements. They must test the principle of meeting-going by its observance, the Word of Wisdom by obeying it, the law of tithing by compliance with it. In this manner only, by putting knowledge into action, can its truth be established.

A person, however clever, who does not do this, not only fails to receive a testimony, but he also loses the right to pass opinion on the principles of the gospel. He cannot judge that which he does not know and has not tried out.

There is nothing new in this principle. Any layman of us may read books on astronomy, and thrill to the order and vastness of the starry heavens as described by others. Only, however, if that knowledge awakens a desire, and touches our wills to make personal exploration of the sky can we become astronomers. The astronomer merges himself in the science. He goes beyond the books, for he looks through the telescope, examines the bands in the spectroscope, and invades in every possible manner the extent and hidden places of the universe. Then, he may indeed bear testimony to astronomy. (*John A. Widtsoe*, IE, May 1945, p. 273.)

D.   Seeking in the Right Places

(3D-1) *You will never get a testimony by reading public magazines.* Study the scriptures; study the teachings of the prophets, the modern prophets. You will never get a testimony of the gospel by reading a public magazine written by someone who doesn't have a testimony. You will never get a testimony studying the literature of the scholars who do not have a testimony. Study the gospel, read the Book of Mormon, read the Doctrine and Covenants, the Pearl of Great Price, and the Bible; read the teachings of the modern prophets, the life of Joseph Smith. Learn, and then obey. (*Marion G. Romney*, BYU, 25 Mar. 1953, p. 7.)

(3D-2) *It is to Him that you should appeal.* "But" says one, "how can you expect men and women to receive these doctrines? We have your testimony; but what other evidence do you have that this is the truth?" We only ask you to place to the test that same request which Jesus made of His disciples and people in His day when He said to them, "My doctrine is not mine, but His that sent me. If any man will do His will, he shall know of the doctrine, whether it be of God, or whether I speak of myself." We say to the people of the world today: "Do not accept our testimony alone. . . . You need not accept the testimony of any man concerning this religion. . . . You can seek the Almighty in your closets. He is not a God that is afar off; not one whose ears are closed, or whose arm is withdrawn from His children; but He is a God whose eye is upon the humblest creature that lives, of every race and color, and whose love is extended to the whole human family. It is to Him that you should appeal for a testimony of the truth of this work which the Lord has established. And if you will do this, in humility and in faith, we have no fear as to the results of your prayers; for God will hear and answer every soul." (*Abraham H. Cannon,* DW, 9 Feb. 1895, p. 226.)

(3D-3) *So why not go directly to God?* When we want bus travel information, we go to the bus terminal; when we want financial assistance, we seek out a banker; so why not go directly to God for a confirming testimony of him and his work? "Ask, and it shall be given you; seek, and ye shall find; knock, and it shall be opened unto you; For every one that asketh receiveth; and he that seeketh findeth; and to him that knocketh it shall be opened. Or what man is there of you, whom if his son ask bread, will he give him a stone? Or if he ask a fish, will he give him a serpent? If ye then . . . know how to give good gifts unto your children, how much more shall your Father which is in heaven give good things to them that ask him?" (Matthew 7:7-11.) (*Robert L. Simpson,* CR, Oct. 1965, p. 78.)

(3D-4) *He is not found in a campus laboratory.* One may acquire knowledge of space and in a limited degree conquer it. He may explore the moon and other planets, but no man can ever really find God in a university campus laboratory, in the physical test tubes of workshops, nor on the testing fields at Cape Kennedy. God and his program will be found only in deep pondering, appropriate reading, much kneeling in devout, humble prayer, and in a sincerity born of need and dependence.

These requirements having been fully met, there is no soul between the poles nor from ocean to ocean who may not positively obtain this knowledge, this hidden treasure of knowledge, this saving and exalting knowledge. (*Spencer W. Kimball,* CR, Oct. 1968, p. 130.)

(3D-5) *They too deserve an honest hearing.* With the great accumulation of knowledge that has been derived through specialization, no single person can grasp all of the learning that is now available to mankind. For this reason man is compelled to rely upon the experience or authority of others for some of his information. Each of us turns to the doctor, the dentist, the lawyer, the teacher, the mechanic, the spiritual leaders, and many other persons for guidance in particular problems. The student of chemistry, for example, does not begin from scratch to rely upon his own experience. He uses the efforts of the teacher, the text, the reference book, and other sources of authority. To bypass such a vast accumulation of knowledge would be folly indeed.

Likewise, in religion we have preserved for us the sayings and teachings and testimonies of Moses, of Amos, of Paul; of Alma in the Book of Mormon; of Joseph Smith in his life and teachings; and of course, of the Christ. These were not persons who were eccentric, but individuals who were significant in stature, living in real life situations, claiming wisdom from God, and bearing personal testimony that these things that are recorded in our scriptures are indeed true. They too deserve an honest hearing. (*Paul H. Dunn,* CR, Apr. 1966, pp. 122-123.)

E.   There Is No Excuse for Not Knowing

(3E-1) *Lack of this knowledge indicates slothfulness and laxness.* I would not give much for a Latter-day Saint who does not know these things, because the want of this knowledge proves that individual slothful and lax; but they who have it are awake and active, ready at all times to put a shoulder to the wheel and aid in rolling forth the great work of the last dispensation; and herein lies the strength of the latter-day work. (*George Q. Cannon,* DW, 7 Mar. 1891, p. 321.)

(3E-2) *If they have lacked that witness it is their fault.* Every Latter-day Saint is entitled to this witness and testimony. If we have not received this witness and testimony . . . I want you all to remember that the fault is ours, and not the Lord's; for every one is entitled to that witness through faith and repentance, forsaking all sin, baptism by immersion for the remission of sins, and the reception of the Holy Ghost through the laying on of hands. Now, if any of our brethren and sisters have lived for years without really knowing, being thoroughly satisfied and thoroughly convinced, just as positive as of anything in life, that this work is of God, if they have lacked that witness and testimony it is their fault, for it is not possible for a man to do the will of the Father and not know the doctrine. (*Francis M. Lyman,* CR, Apr. 1910, pp. 29-30.)

(3E-3) *We have no one to blame except ourselves.* Is there any good reason why every living soul cannot know the truth and where it can be found? Is there any reason that any members of this Church can give why he does not know that Jesus Christ is the Son of God, that Joseph Smith was and is a prophet of God, and that this is his work? If we lack that understanding, we have no one to blame but ourselves. I had perfect confidence in the sayings of the Lord and Savior, Jesus Christ; and when he says, 'Ask and it shall be given you; seek and ye shall find; knock, and it shall be opened unto you. For everyone that asketh receiveth,' I am just as sure that every member of this Church may know within himself or herself that God lives, Jesus Christ is the Son of God, and that this is his work which he has established. We have no excuse whatever for not knowing and having the absolute faith and confidence in this restored gospel of Jesus Christ. It is our duty to know. (*Joseph Fielding Smith,* CR, Apr. 1951, p. 59.)

(3E-4) *The error is in doing nothing about it.* And now to those who by heritage find themselves members of the Church but perhaps are not sure of their own testimony — to you I would suggest that it is no sin to admit to yourself that you do not know if, in fact, you don't know. The error might be, however, in coming to the realization that you don't know and then doing nothing about it. Any person, either member or nonmember, who wants to know *can* know. If at present you live by the faith and testimony of your parents and those around you, that is certainly all right. But seek to reach out and gain your own testimony so you can stand on the strength of your own personal relationship with the Lord. It will help you in solving many of your problems and bring peace to your heart. (*Loren C. Dunn,* CR, Oct. 1972, p. 97.)

(3E-5) *Failure in our method.* By prayer and right living, and conformity to gospel teachings, every soul is entitled to and will receive this knowledge and testimony. If we do not succeed in getting it, there is failure in our method. (*George Albert Smith,* IE, Feb. 1925, p. 390.)

F.   There Are No Shortcuts to a Testimony

(3F-1) *Rules for a testimony the same regardless of learning.* A friend of mine outside the Church said to me in New York City a few weeks ago: "I believe 'Mormonism' to be true, I regard it as a sound philosophy, but I do not know that Joseph Smith was a prophet. If not a prophet," my friend added, "he was certainly the most marvelous thinker of modern times, but I have no testimony that he was specially sent from God." I asked him how he could expect to have such a testimony unless he obeyed the Gospel, unless he took the course which the Lord has pointed out whereby men may lay hold upon divine knowledge. He is an honest man, a man of intelligence and culture, with no less than eight languages at his tongue's end, and is apparently versed in all the learning of our time; but he does not know what you and I know — we who have so little of his learning, and yet possess something inestimably greater, a testimony of the truth. If he ever arrives at the knowledge which you and I possess it will be when he has obeyed the same principles that you and I have obeyed. . . . And this way is open to all; the king upon his throne or the peasant in his cot may have it if he so desires; but there is only one way for the king or for the peasant. When it comes to candidacy for salvation, for citizenship in the kingdom of heaven, all men are equal — they get salvation and glory upon precisely the same terms. (*Orson F. Whitney*, CR, Oct. 1914, p. 83.)

(3F-2) *It cannot be purchased.* To a Latter-day Saint, a testimony of the truthfulness of the restored gospel is the most precious possession he can have. It cannot be purchased. No one can give it to him. It can only be secured by prayer, by study, by faith, by repentance, by righteous living, and by listening to others bearing their testimonies, and through the manifestation of the Holy Ghost. (*O. Leslie Stone*, CR, Apr. 1975, pp. 9-10.)

(3F-3) *There are not two ways, only one way.* There is no shortcut to a testimony. There are not two ways. There is only one. The Lord revealed that sure and certain way when he said: "Oliver Cowdery, verily, verily, I say unto you that assuredly as the Lord liveth, who is your God and your Redeemer, even so surely shall you receive a knowledge of whatsoever things you shall ask in faith, with an honest heart, believing that you shall receive a knowledge. . . . Yea, behold, I will tell you in your mind and in your heart, by the Holy Ghost, which shall come upon you and which shall dwell in your heart. Now, behold, this is the spirit of revelation. . . ." (Doctrine and Covenants 8:1-3.)

Everyone who sincerely prays with real desire to know concerning what he has learned about the gospel, will receive a witness, "in [his] mind and in [his] heart, by the Holy Ghost," as the Lord said to Oliver. And, as the Lord said, this witness "shall dwell in [his] heart." And it shall dwell in his heart forever if he retains his faith by (1) repenting of his sins, (2) being baptized, (3) receiving the gift of the Holy Ghost by the laying on of hands, and (4) continuing to obey the principles of the gospel to the end of his mortal life. (*Marion G. Romney*, ACR, Aug. 1975 — Tokyo, Japan, pp. 47-48.)

(3F-4) A *gift for everyone, not just a select few.* A firm and abiding testimony of this great latter-day work is not reserved for your bishopric and a select group of high priests in the ward. A testimony of the truth is a free gift from God to everyone who is willing to go through the process of building a testimony. . . .

Anyone can acquire this testimony by following the established procedure by which the Lord gives a testimony. There are no shortcuts. A desire to know is imperative. To learn the doctrine is essential. To do his will will sanctify that teaching in your heart. To pray often will open the way and make all things possible through him, for he has said, " . . . without me ye can do nothing." (John 15:5.) (*Robert L. Simpson*, NE, Mar. 1972, pp. 4, 6.)

4

THE RECEIPT
OF A TESTIMONY

A.   Ways in Which a Testimony May Come

(4A-1) *It need not be a dramatic, emotional event.* After you have studied the gospel diligently, conformed your life to the principles taught therein, and asked God in prayer to confirm the truth of the restoration of the gospel, then you must be able to recognize the answer from the Lord when it comes.

Many believe that a testimony comes as a dramatic, emotional event. But more often than not, a testimony comes as a feeling that the gospel is true. And while it may be an unexplainable experience, it is real. The Lord has described the feeling that comes in this way: " . . . you shall feel that it is right." (Doctrine and Covenants 9:8.)

The Lord spoke to Oliver Cowdery on one occasion regarding the power and reality of this experience. He said: "Verily, verily, I say unto you, if you desire a further witness, cast your mind upon the night that you cried unto me in your heart, that you might know concerning the truth of these things. Did I not speak peace to your mind concerning the matter? What greater witness can you have than from God?" (Doctrine and Covenants 6:22-23.) (*John H. Vandenberg,* IE, Dec. 1968, p. 111.)

(4A-2) *When your heart tells you things your mind does not know.* A young missionary spoke to me in the temple yesterday, after we had had an hour or so of questions, and said, "I represent these missionaries in telling you we have respect for you, but will you tell us something that will strengthen our testimonies and make us better prepared to go out as missionaries?"

I responded by saying, "Well, let me share with you an experience I had with one of our business executives. His wife and children are members, but he is not. His twin sons are attending Brigham Young University, and one of them is planning to be married in the temple next year. But he said to me, 'I can't join the Church until I get a testimony.' I said to him, 'The next time you are in Salt Lake, come in and visit with me.' As we talked following our business meeting a few weeks later I said to him, 'I don't know if you realize whether you have a testimony or not; or if you know what a testimony is.' And so he wanted to know what a testimony is. I answered him by saying, 'When the time comes that your heart tells you things your mind doesn't know, that is the Spirit of the Lord dictating to you.' And then I said, 'As I've come to know you, there are things that you know in your heart are true. No angel is going to tap you on the shoulder and tell you this is true.' " The Spirit of the Lord is as the Master said: "The wind bloweth where it listeth, and thou hearest the sound thereof, but canst not tell whence it cometh, and whither it goeth; so is every one that is born of the Spirit." (John 3:8.)

So I said to my friend, the business executive: "Now, remember that your testimony won't come in a dramatic way, but when it comes, the tears of gladness will water your pillow by night. You'll know, my beloved friend, when that testimony comes." (*Harold B. Lee*, BYU, 1973, pp. 100-101.)

(4A-3) *Physical manifestations are not the only source of testimony.* I listened as a boy to a testimony regarding the principles of the gospel, the power of the priesthood, the divinity of this work. I heard the admonition that we, too, might get that testimony if we would pray, but somehow I got an idea in youth that we could not get a testimony unless we had some manifestation. I read of the First Vision of the Prophet Joseph Smith, and I knew that he knew what he had received was of God; I heard of elders who had heard voices; I heard my father's testimony of a voice that had come to him declaring the divinity of the mission of the Prophet, and somehow I received the impression that that was the source of all testimony.

I realized in youth that the most precious thing that a man could obtain in this life was a testimony of the divinity of this work. I hungered for it; I felt that if I could get that, all else would indeed seem insignificant. I did not neglect my prayers, but I never felt that my prayer at night would bring that testimony; that was more a prayer for protection, as I look back upon it now, to keep intruders away — really it was more of a selfish prayer — but I always felt that the secret prayer, whether in the room or out in the grove or on the hills, would be the place where that much-desired testimony would come.

Accordingly, I have knelt more than once by the serviceberry bush, as my saddle horse stood by the side. I remember riding over the hills one afternoon, thinking of these things, and concluded that there in the silence of the hills was the best place to get that testimony. I stopped my horse, threw the reins over his head, and withdrew just a few steps and knelt by the side of a tree.

The air was clear and pure, the sunshine delightful; the verdure of the wild trees and grass and the flowers scented the air; as I recall the incident, all the surroundings come to me anew. I knelt down and with all the fervor of my heart poured out my soul to God and asked him for a testimony of the gospel. I had in mind that there would be some manifestation, that I should receive some transformation that would leave me without doubt.

I arose, mounted my horse, and as he started over the trail I remember rather introspectively searching myself, and involuntarily shaking my head, said to myself, "No sir, there is no change; I am just the same boy I was before I knelt down." The anticipated manifestation had not come.

Nor was that the only occasion. However, it did come, but not in the way I had anticipated. Even the manifestation of God's power and the presence of his angels came, but when it did come, it was simply a confirmation; it was not the testimony. . . .

But the testimony that this work is divine had come, not through manifestation, great and glorious as it was, but through obedience to God's will, in harmony with Christ's promise, "If any man will do his will, he will know of the doctrine, whether it be of God, or whether I speak of myself." (John 7:17.)

Test it from any source you wish, and you will find that there is not one phase of the gospel of Jesus Christ which will not stand that test; and as you, in your weakness, as you in your youth, undertake to embrace these principles of life everlasting, you will find it instilling upon your soul a benediction of the Holy Spirit which will give you a testimony beyond any possibility of a doubt that God lives, that he is indeed our Father and that this is his work established through the Prophet Joseph Smith. (*David O. McKay*, IE, Sept. 1962, pp. 628-629.)

(4A-4) *It may not come in the way we desire.* [A] . . . testimony is within the reach of everyone. God has said that none who seek Him shall be turned away unsatisfied. Sometimes the testimony does not come in the way that we have desired. We do not receive the outward manifestations which we have been led to expect. But it is not the outward appearances, it is not the healing of the sick, nor the hearing of tongues, that gives a man or woman the greatest strength in the work of God; for those who have seen angels, whose eyes have not been closed to the glories of eternity, and to whom it has seemed impossible for God to forbid even anything which they asked — they have turned away from the truth, lost the testimony of the Spirit, and again gone into darkness. Better by far for us to possess is the still small voice of the Spirit — the inward feeling which is experienced in every fibre of our organization, which tingles in our veins, which reaches the extremities of our bodies, and tells our whole being that this is the work of God. (*Abraham H. Cannon*, DW, 16 June 1894, pp. 801-802.)

(4A-5) *The type of testimony the Lord blessed.* There are two kinds of testimony, one which comes from the senses, the eye, the ear, the touch. So far as I am concerned, because I know how uncertain is the eye and the ear and the touch, I have felt that the other testimony, the testimony of the Spirit, was for me the truer one.

As for the testimony of the senses, you will remember that Thomas, one of the Lord's ancient Apostles, was not present at the meeting on the evening of the day of the resurrection when Christ appeared to the others. They, when he appeared, had not believed until he had by his presence and his words and actions shown them that he was actually the risen Lord. When Thomas was told of this, he said he would not believe " . . . Except I shall see in his hands the print of the nails, and put my finger into the print of the nails, and thrust my hand into his side." (John 20:25.)

The week following that first meeting, the disciples were together again. Thomas was there also. Suddenly into the room came Jesus, even as he had come the week before; he turned to Thomas and said: "Reach hither thy finger, and behold my hands; and reach hither thy hand, and thrust it into my side; and be not faithless, but believing." Thomas, beholding the Lord, said: "My Lord and my God."

And then the Savior said unto him: "Thomas, because thou hast seen me, thou hast believed: blessed are they that have not seen, and yet have believed." (John 20:27, 28, 29.)

And that is the testimony of the Christ which must come to most of us, the testimony of believing without seeing, a testimony which the Lord blessed. And this testimony is the testimony of the Spirit. . . . We should all seek for it. If the Lord wishes to add the testimony of the senses, we should be grateful; but the testimony of the spirit is within the call of all of us. All we need to do to get it is to live for it and seek it; and that testimony when it comes will be in us a burning testimony, a testimony that will be as a fire, if we so live that we keep it. We should see to it that it is fed by righteous works, proper living. We should see to it that it never becomes smothered by the ashes of transgression. (*J. Reuben Clark, Jr.*, IE, Aug. 1949, pp. 495, 539-540.)

(4A-6) *More than likely it will come in a rather calm, natural but real way.* The best way to get a testimony — and most of you have heard the words all your lives — is through the Book of Mormon. I know of no greater way to establish that relationship with the Lord than through the pages of the Book of Mormon — to read, ponder, pray. . . . It may not come like a flash of light (I don't know how the Lord is going to communicate with you), more than likely it will be the reassurance and a feeling in your heart, a reaffirmation that will come in a rather calm, natural but real way from day to day until you come to a realization that you *do* know, and that you know in a way that nobody could really tell you, because it is not just something that comes to your mind. It involves the whole being. (*Loren C. Dunn*, UU, 10 Nov. 1972, p. 5.)

(4A-7) *Revelation, not miracles, should be the base of a testimony.* One way of gaining a testimony is through miracles. I heard . . . of a nurse who had been told that a patient would die so far as the skill of doctors was concerned, for physicians had so concluded. Two . . . Elders administered to the patient, and she or he recovered. Observing the result of the administration the nurse had said to somebody, "I know now that this is the true gospel." But did she?

What she really did know was that that young man or woman was healed by a blessing. Whether that patient was cured through his or her own faith or the faith of the Elders or the power of the Priesthood, she does not know. . . . I remind you of the frequent warnings in the New Testament given by the Savior after his having performed a miracle. "See thou tellest no man." There was something more convincing than miracles regarding the testimony of his divinity which the Savior was trying to get his disciples to realize. . . . Peter and other disciples were present when Peter's mother-in-law was healed, when the blind received their sight, when the ten lepers came, they also saw the widow's only son at Nain restored to life. But greater than all these evidences was something which Christ was waiting to be developed within souls of his disciples and particularly within the heart of that practical man, Simon, son of Jonas. For nearly two years Christ watched for that development. . . . It did not come suddenly to Peter. Let me call your attention to one instance.

After feeding the 5,000, you remember, the Savior crossed over to Capernaum on that tempestuous sea. Some of the 5,000 walked around the northern shore and were in Capernaum to meet him the next day. Whether the Savior gave his address in the streets of Capernaum or in the synagogue, he delivered a masterful message, in which he said to the assembled multitude, "Ye seek me, not because ye saw the glory of God, but because ye ate of the loaves and were filled." They had seen the miracle but they had missed something deeper, more significant.

Then Jesus delivered that remarkable sermon on the bread of life, but its symbolism they could not understand and began to walk away. Those who had followed him began to leave him, and turn their backs upon him, and finally only the Twelve were left unto whom he said, "Will ye also go away?" Peter, the impulsive leader, practical and sound spokesman (I love him!), said unto him: "To whom shall we go, Lord? Thou hast the words of eternal life and we believe and are sure thou art the Christ, the Son of the Living God."

I lingered on *believe* and *are sure* because I think that is the way Peter said it. It seemed that at that time Peter's testimony was not strong and definite. I may be wrong and do not ask you to accept that interpretation if you do not believe it, but of this we may be sure, on that occasion he did not get the word "blessed."

Jesus took the disciples from Capernaum and went up into the mountain close by to teach them further, and it was while he was up there during that week that he asked the question, "Whom do men say that I am?" They answered and said, "Some say that thou are Elias, and others Jeremiah, and others say John the Baptist." Then he said, "Whom do ye say that I am?" And Peter, answered without hesitation. "Thou art the Christ, the Son of the Living God."

"Blessed art thou, Simon Bar-jona, for flesh and blood hath not revealed it unto thee, but my Father which is in heaven. And I say also unto thee, thou art Peter [Peter saw this testimony or revelation from God], and upon this rock I will build my Church; and the gates of hell shall not prevail against it."

Inspiration, revelation to the individual soul is the rock upon which a testimony should be built and there is not one living who cannot get it if he will conform to those laws and live a clean life which will permit the Holy Spirit to place that testimony in him. (*David O. McKay, CN,* 12 Sept. 1951, pp. 2, 4.)

(4A-8) *A stupor or a burning are not the only ways in which God can tell us.* Now, clearly, the word of Christ, as given in the past through the holy scriptures and as given to us now through the Holy Ghost, can provide us with the guidance necessary to help us to know "all things that [we] should do." (2 Nephi 32:3.) Such can happen when the Holy Ghost is our constant companion, not a periodic partner.

There is a twin danger in our glossing over certain promises as profound as this one, however. First, we may be unduly harsh on ourselves when revelations for our personal lives do not gush forth as if from a fire hydrant. Second, we may think of the process as if it were like switching our decision-making apparatus on "automatic pilot," leaving us with a ho-hum role.

We must make allowance for the real possibility that we are lacking in faith and/or worthiness. But we must also make allowance for the equally real possibility that some considerations of growth are involved at times, too. Oliver Cowdery was told that he had oversimplified his role in the process: "You took no thought save it was to ask." (Doctrine and Covenants 9:7.)

Next, the effort to study propositions out in our mind, carefully and prayerfully, can be followed by a stupor or a burning, but these are not the only ways in which God can tell what we should do. There is a spectrum of styles used by the Lord to inspire and guide us. If we seek to make the process too mechanical, we may deprive ourselves of guidance from God that comes in other ways, equally valid. . . .

Inspiration can come in the form of our being directed to already revealed wisdom that is apropos and adequate for our need. The disciple needs to become at home in the Lord's library. A bit of wisdom or a phrase uttered by a friend in a timely way can remain in our mind and prove catalytic in meeting the later challenge. (*Neal A. Maxwell*, WPF, pp. 119-121.)

(4A-9) *It is not easy to explain to the uninitiated.* The Holy Ghost is the third member of the Trinity. He is, as has already been said, "a personage of Spirit." (Doctrine and Covenants 130:22.) One of his functions is to bear witness of the Father and the Son to the honest, believing truth seeker.

In harmony with the Lord's promises, every soul who will acquaint himself with the testimonies of the prophets concerning God and then ask him "in the name of Christ, . . . with a sincere heart, with real intent, having faith in Christ," if these testimonies are true, will receive a manifestation "by the power of the Holy Ghost" that they are true. (Moroni 10:4.)

It is not easy to explain to the uninitiated how this witness comes. Speaking about it to Nicodemus, Jesus said: "The wind bloweth where it listeth, and thou hearest the sound thereof, but canst not tell whence it cometh, and whither it goeth: so is every one that is born of the Spirit." (John 3:8.)

In 1829, the Lord gave this explanation to Oliver Cowdery as to how the witness of the Spirit comes: "Behold, you have not understood; you have supposed that I would give it unto you, when you took no thought save it was to ask me. But, behold, I say unto you, that you must study it out in your mind; then you must ask me if it be right, and if it is right I will cause that your bosom shall burn within you; therefore, you shall feel that it is right." (Doctrine and Covenants 9:7-8.)

On another occasion, he said to Oliver Cowdery: "Verily, verily, I say unto you, if you desire a further witness, cast your mind upon the night that you cried unto me in your heart, that you might know concerning the truth of these things." He was then trying to find out for himself whether or not the Prophet had the plates as he said he had. And then the Lord continued: "Did I not speak peace to your mind concerning the matter? What greater witness can you have than from God?" (Doctrine and Covenants 6:22-23.)

He whose desire to know the living God is strong enough to induce him to follow the prescribed course can and will get the witness for himself. And then he will understand what the Lord was saying in these scriptures. However, he who does not so seek will never understand these revelations, nor the revelations which God has given of himself.

One who receives the witness of the Holy Ghost has a sure knowledge that God lives; that he is our Father in heaven; that Jesus Christ is our Elder Brother in the spirit and the Only Begotten of the Father in the flesh, our Savior and Redeemer. Such a one knows that the universal order in the heavens above, in the earth beneath, and in the waters under the earth, all give evidence that God lives; he knows that the testimonies of the prophets concerning the Father, Son, and Holy Ghost are accurate and true. Secure in this knowledge, his life has purpose. The gospel of Jesus Christ becomes for him what Paul said it is: "The power of God unto salvation." (Romans 1:16.) (*Marion G. Romney*, CR, Oct. 1967, pp. 136-137.)

(4A-10) *Do you expect the Lord to get a club and knock you down?* As I sit here today, I remember what to me was one of the greatest of all the incidents in my life, in this tabernacle. One Sunday afternoon, nearly fifty years ago, I came here as one of the youngest of the apostles to attend the meeting, and saw for the first time in the congregation, my brother who had been careless, indifferent, and wayward, and who had evinced no interest in the Gospel of Jesus Christ. . . . [Realizing] that he was seeking God for light and knowledge regarding the divinity of this work, I bowed my head and I prayed . . . the Lord would inspire me by the revelation of His Spirit, to speak in such a manner that my brother would have to acknowledge to me that I had spoken beyond my natural ability, that I had been inspired by the Lord.

I realized that if he made that confession, then I should be able to point out to him that God had given him a testimony of the divinity of this work. . . .

I devoted my thirty minutes almost entirely to a testimony of my knowledge that God lives, that Jesus is the Christ, and to the wonderful and marvelous labors of the Prophet Joseph Smith, bearing witness to the knowledge God had given me that Joseph Smith was in very deed a prophet of the true and living God. . . .

The next morning, my brother came into my office and said, "Heber, I was at a meeting yesterday and heard you preach."

I said, "The first time you ever heard your brother preach, I guess?"

"Oh, no," he said, "I have heard you many times. I generally come in late and go into the gallery. I often go out before the meeting is over. But you never spoke as you did yesterday. You spoke beyond your natural ability. You were inspired of the Lord." These were the identical words I had uttered the day before, in my prayer to the Lord!

I said to him, "Are you still praying for a testimony of the Gospel?"

He said, "Yes, and I am going nearly wild."

I asked, "What did I preach about yesterday?"

He replied, "You know what you preached about."

I said, "Well, you tell me."

"You preached upon the divine mission of the Prophet Joseph Smith."

I answered, "And I was inspired beyond my natural ability; and I never spoke before at any time you have heard me, as I spoke yesterday. Do you expect the Lord to get a club and knock you down? What more testimony do you want of the Gospel of Jesus Christ than that a man speaks beyond his natural ability and under the inspiration of God, when he testifies of the divine mission of the Prophet Joseph Smith?"

The next Sabbath he applied to me for baptism. (*Heber J. Grant,* CR, Apr. 1944, pp. 4-7, 9.)

B.   The Testimony of Greatest Value

(4B-1) *The impressions made by the Holy Ghost can be equally deep and lasting.* Joseph Smith, although only a youth, had faith and prayed to our Heavenly Father for an answer to a problem which was of sincere concern to him. He was blessed with a personal visitation from our Father in heaven and the Lord Jesus Christ.

Saul of Tarsus, who was a persecutor of the followers of Jesus, became

Paul the apostle, defender of the Christ, following a dramatic experience while on the road to Damascus. A light was seen in the heavens, and he heard a voice saying, "Saul, Saul, why persecutest thou me?" And he answered and said, "Who art thou, Lord?" And the Lord replied: "I am Jesus whom thou persecutest: it is hard for thee to kick against the pricks." (Acts 9:3-5.)

These two incidents were rare manifestations, but the impressions made by the Holy Ghost can be equally deep and lasting. President Joseph Fielding Smith has said, "Therefore, the seeing, even the Savior, does not leave as deep an impression in the mind as does the testimony of the Holy Ghost to the spirit. . . . The impressions on the soul that come from the Holy Ghost are far more significant than a vision. It is where spirit speaks to spirit, and the imprint upon the soul is far more difficult to erase." (*Seek Ye Earnestly,* pages 213-214.)

This truth is further illustrated by the experiences of the three witnesses to the Book of Mormon. Each of the three — Oliver Cowdery, David Whitmer, and Martin Harris — saw the angel, saw and handled the gold plates from which the Book of Mormon was translated, and heard the voice of the Lord declare that the record was true. Yet later, all three, becoming disaffected and out of harmony with the leaders, dwindled in unbelief and apostasy. But the imprint of the Spirit had been so indelible that not a single one of them ever denied his testimony, which is still printed in each copy of the Book of Mormon. The testimony of the still small voice whispering to our innermost beings is of more worth than outward signs or manifestations. (*Henry D. Taylor,* CR, Apr. 1971, p. 159.)

(4B-2) *More important than sight is the witness of the Spirit.* I repeat to you . . . something President Grant once said that rather startled me. He said he had heard of men who declared that they had had a personal visitation from the Lord. And then President Grant added, "Some of those who had that experience lost their testimonies. It seemed that they became puffed up in the pride of their hearts, perhaps thinking that they were more special to the Lord than others who had not received the same experience. . . . "

As I have thought of that, I am sobered by it. As I pray for the guidance of the Spirit . . . I ask only to go where the Lord would have me go, and only to receive what the Lord would have me receive, knowing that more important than sight is the witness that one may have by the witness of the Holy Ghost to his soul that things are so and that Jesus is the Christ, a living personage. (*Harold B. Lee,* BYU, 1973, pp. 87-88.)

(4B-3) *A witness far greater than seeing the Lord.* We are Special Witnesses, called to bear witness to the life and mission of our Redeemer.

There are people in the Church, a few I suppose, I have heard of some of them, who raise a question about our worthiness to act in these callings. They hold to the view, which is held to some extent in the Protestant world, that men cannot be special witnesses and apostles of Jesus Christ, who have not seen him. I remember one time at a stake conference, when a good brother was called on to speak and he made this statement. I think his remarks were aimed at me and most of the other brethren who were in this council at that time. He said that there was only one member of the Council of the Twelve who was qualified to be an Apostle, that was Elder Ballard, because he had seen the Lord. So the rest of the council were counted out. Of course I had the opportunity to follow this brother and make some remarks and correct this statement.

When I spoke I read the words of our Savior as recorded in Matthew, chapter 12, verses 31 and 32. They are as follows: "Wherefore I say unto you, all manner of sin and blasphemy shall be forgiven unto men; but the blasphemy against the Holy Ghost shall not be forgiven unto men. And whosoever speaketh a word against the Son of man, it shall be forgiven him: but whosoever speaketh against the Holy Ghost, it shall not be forgiven him, neither in this world, neither in the world to come."

I impressed upon the minds of that congregation that there was a witness far greater than seeing the Lord. A man might see him in a vision and turn away, deny him, and sin against his name, but for him should he truly repent, there would be forgiveness, but denial of Jesus Christ and the blasphemy against the Holy Ghost, after a man had received that testimony of the Spirit, could not be forgiven in this world, neither in the world to come. The assurance that comes from the Spirit, which penetrates the soul and gives the assurance that Jesus Christ is the Son of God and our Redeemer, is more powerful and penetrating than a vision which may be seen and then in course of time be forgotten. Then I asked the congregation which was the greater, the testimony of seeing where the vision in course of time becomes dim, or to receive the penetrating influence of the Spirit of God which penetrates the soul — constantly reassuring.

Every member of the Council of the Twelve, I feel sure, could testify by the power of the Holy Ghost, that Jesus Christ is the Redeemer of the world, and in order to be an Apostle, with all the power and authority and knowledge necessary did not depend upon having a vision, but it did depend upon the testimony that comes from the source of testimony — the third member of the Godhead. (*Joseph Fielding Smith,* MI, pp. 125-127.)

(4B-4) *The greatest kind of testimony.* Anything that furnishes evidence that this is God's work, is a testimony concerning it. But healings are not the greatest evidence, they are but parts of a supreme testimony, greater than dreams, visions, prophecies, healings, tongues, and all other manifestations combined. The greatest of all testimonies is the illumination of the soul by the gift and power of the Holy Ghost. (*Orson F. Whitney,* CR, Apr. 1930, p. 135.)

(4B-5) *The witness of the Spirit is still necessary.* Although Peter walked and talked with the Savior and had observed many of his miracles, yet when he said, "Thou art the Christ, the Son of the living God," the Savior pointed out that it wasn't flesh and blood that revealed this to Peter, but his Father in heaven.

This tells us that there is a more certain way of knowing than actually seeing with our eyes; for there were many who saw Jesus Christ but knew him not as the Son of God. Those that did know him knew him because it was revealed to them by our Father in heaven.

The witness of the Spirit is mentioned in Luke, chapter twenty-four, as two of the disciples were walking along the road to a village called Emmaus. The Savior himself came and walked and talked with them, but they did "not know him" until right at the very end when their eyes were opened and they knew him. Verse 32 says: "And they said one to another, Did not our heart burn within us, while he talked with us by the way, and while he opened to us the scriptures?"

With all the logic and outward evidences of the truthfulness of the gospel, it still comes down to the witness of the Spirit.

"Did not our heart burn within us?" is as applicable today to a person seeking the gospel of Jesus Christ as it was during the time of Christ .... (*Loren C. Dunn*, CR, Apr. 1977, pp. 42-43.)

(4B-6) *We can always trust spiritual promptings.* We were reminded last Thursday in our meeting in the temple prior to this conference that the greatest testimony is that which comes and testifies of the Spirit. We cannot always trust what we see and what we hear, but we can always trust that prompting of the Spirit that comes to us, which declares to us that which is truth; and by that power we get our strength and testimony of the gospel of Jesus Christ. (*Eldred G. Smith*, CR, Oct. 1956, p. 76.)

(4B-7) *There is no greater testimony given to any man.* Now, if you have the Holy Ghost with you, . . . I can say unto you that there is no greater gift, there is no greater blessing, there is no greater testimony given to any man on earth. You may have the administration of angels; you may see many miracles; you may see many wonders in the earth; but I claim that the gift of the Holy Ghost is the greatest gift that can be bestowed upon man. (*Wilford Woodruff*, DW, 6 Apr. 1889, p. 451.)

C.   Not Knowing That You Know

(4C-1) *It may be only "this" big.* Sometimes, as I interview missionaries, I say, "Do you want to go on a mission?" "Yes!" "Why do you want to go?" "Well, I haven't any testimony, but I think it's something I would like to do." And I say, "Of course, you have a testimony! You wouldn't go out and preach for Catholicism, would you? Suppose a Methodist minister asked you to go out and preach Methodism for two years, would you? Of course you wouldn't! But you would go out and preach Mormonism. Therefore, you do have a testimony! It may be only "this" big ... but you *do* have a testimony or you wouldn't go preaching the Gospel." (*Spencer W. Kimball*, UA-CHD, 2 Jan. 1959 — Los Angeles, Calif., pp. 3-4.)

(4C-2) *People who do not know that they know.* Now, we . . . [have] . . . people that know, but don't know they know. We had a situation in Church history where . . . Heber J. Grant . . . was sent out to Tooele Stake . . . to be stake president. He was a young man. They had a lot of good men out in Tooele Stake, but somehow a man was imported in to be their stake president. Now, this didn't strike the people of Tooele too well at first. Not only that, when he got up to give his first address at stake conference (and as I understand it, the President of the Church at that time came out to install him), he only spoke for a few minutes and at the end of his address he said, "I think the Church is true." After the meeting some of the members cornered the President of the Church and said, "Not only do you bring in a person from outside, but he is not even sure the Church is true." The President of the Church chuckled and said, "Oh, President Grant knows the Church is true, all right. He just doesn't know that he knows." And between that conference and the next conference President Grant established his relationship with the Lord, and when he spoke the next time it was for forty-five minutes, and by the power and spirit of God.

Too many times, when it is a part of our heritage, we don't always know what it is to be without it, and sometimes we talk ourselves into thinking that we don't have a testimony because it is so much a part of our lives we don't always recognize it. And so we need to ask these questions of ourselves, and if there are any doubts, then go through the same process to either gain that witness and testimony or have it reaffirmed to our hearts. (*Loren C. Dunn, UU*, 10 Nov. 1972, pp. 5-6.)

(4C-3) *Many people do not recognize that they carry a testimony.* Many people carry . . . a testimony in their own lives and do not recognize its worth. Recently a young lady said, "I do not have a testimony of the gospel. I wish I did. I accept its teachings. I know they work in my life. I see them working in the lives of others. If only the Lord would answer my prayers and give me a testimony, I would be one of the happiest persons alive!" What this young lady wanted was a miraculous intervention; yet she had already seen the miracle of the gospel enlarging and uplifting her own life. The Lord *had* answered her prayers. She *did* have a testimony, but she did not recognize it for what it was. Of such, Jesus said,". . . they seeing see not; and hearing they hear not, neither do they understand." (Matthew 13:13.) (*Howard W. Hunter,* CR, Apr. 1967, p. 116.)

(4C-4) *Adversity and a testimony.* A young man, living near Salt Lake City, left for a mission in the Southern States a few years ago. Before he left he said to his mother: "If I do not receive a testimony before I have been in the mission one month, I am going to return home." The mother sweetly answered: "My son, you have a testimony. My prayers will ascend unto God that you will be made conscious of that testimony before you have been in the mission field a month." The young man was put to labor in the Georgia conference. Three weeks after he arrived there, he and his companion were chased by a mob of angry men. The elders discarded their mission grips. They found that their coats impeded their flight, and they threw them aside; but when they had outdistanced their pursuers this young man who had told his mother he would return home within a month if he did not receive a testimony of the truth of the Gospel, shook his fist in the direction of the mob and said: "I know this Gospel is true." But it took a mob to make him conscious of his testimony. — "Sweet are the uses of adversity." (*Charles A. Callis,* CR, Apr. 1929, p. 23.)

(4C-5) *Spiritual gold mines: latent and undeveloped.* I have never done a wiser or better thing [than accept a mission call]. If there is anything in my life that looks like success, it is because I decided as I did at that time. . . .

I know now that I had a testimony, a deep conviction of the Truth; but it was latent, undeveloped, like a gold mine in the depths of the earth. Something had to occur to bring it out. That something was my mission. It bored the tunnel, sunk the shaft, and brought the precious ore to the surface.

I cannot but believe that in the heart of every "Mormon" boy and every "Mormon" girl there is a spiritual gold mine, awaiting development. To some, the development comes early; to others, late. But come it will, sometime, somewhere. They are children of the Covenant; in their veins is the blood of Israel; and they have received, if baptized, the gift of the Holy Ghost, which manifests the things of God. How could all that go for naught? (*Orson F. Whitney,* TMH, p. 68.)

D. A Testimony May Not Come All at Once

(4D-1) *A testimony may come by degrees.* Sometimes . . . [a testimony] . . . comes to a person all of a sudden. He gets it at a certain time, and he knows that he has received it. . . . Sometimes a testimony comes to a person slowly, over an extended period of time. I personally do not remember of a testimony coming to me suddenly. . . .

But whether a testimony comes all of a sudden or whether it comes by degrees, it does something to a person. One is different after he receives a testimony than he was before he received it. Good men, great men, are different. Peter, himself, was different. . . . The experiences of Alma and Paul are also examples of how testimonies change men. My father used to tell me that the difference between a man when he has a testimony and when he does not have one is the difference between a living, growing tree and a dry, dead stump. I am sure he was right. (*Marion G. Romney*, ACR, Aug. 1975 — Tokyo, Japan, pp. 46-47.)

(4D-2) *The full-bloom rose was once an unopened bud.* The youth of the Church may sometimes wonder if they have a testimony. They may ask how it may be obtained. Some young people may be discouraged, and they may compare their knowledge and testimony with that of others, but let me plead with the young people never to become discouraged. Always remember that the full-bloom rose was once an unopened bud and that the ripened fruit was once just a blossom and that all great things came from small beginnings. . . .

Oh, a testimony does not all come at once, but if continually developed and cultivated, it is a power and a strength that will be felt forever. (*Thorpe B. Isaacson*, CR, Oct. 1952, p. 65.)

(4D-3) *Little by little it will be obtained.* When I as a boy first started out in the ministry I would frequently go out and ask the Lord to show me some marvelous thing, in order that I might receive a testimony. But the Lord withheld marvels from me, and showed me the truth, line upon line, precept upon precept, here a little and there a little, until he made me to know the truth from the crown of my head to the soles of my feet, and until doubt and fear had been absolutely purged from me. He did not have to send an angel from the heavens to do this, nor did He have to speak with the trump of an archangel. By the whisperings of the still small voice of the Spirit of the living God, He gave to me the testimony I possess. And by this principle and power He will give to all the children of men a knowledge of the truth that will stay with them, and it will make them to know the truth, as God knows it, and to do the will of the Father as Christ does it. And no amount of marvelous manifestations will ever accomplish this. (*Joseph F. Smith*, CR, Apr. 1900, pp. 40-41.)

(4D-4) *Pretty soon he is nearing the top of the mountain.* The child grows from childhood to boyhood, and from boyhood to manhood, with a constant and steady growth; but he cannot tell how or when the growth occurs. He does not realize that he is growing; but by observing the laws of health and being prudent in his course he eventually arrives at manhood. So in reference to ourselves as Latter-day Saints. We grow and increase. We are not aware of it at the moment; but after a year or so we discover that we are, so to speak, away up the hill, nearing the mountain top. (*Lorenzo Snow*, CR, Apr. 1899, p. 2.)

(4D-5) *Spiritual knowledge will come one step at a time.* It is not wisdom that we should have all knowledge at once presented before us; but that we should have a little at a time; then we can comprehend it. (*Joseph Smith*, HC, Vol. 5, p. 387.)

(4D-6) *A testimony of the gospel is a composite of many testimonies.* I have never been convinced in my mind that a person could get a testimony of the gospel without effort on his part. I think we can get a conviction of a kind that the gospel is true, but I have the peculiar idea that a testimony of the gospel is a composite of many testimonies. I believe that you don't get a testimony of tithing until you live the law of tithing. I don't believe you get a testimony of prayer until you pray. I don't belive you get a testimony of the Book of Mormon until you read and study the Book of Mormon as Moroni said we should, and then ask God whether it is true. Then we get a testimony of it. I don't believe we get a testimony of the Doctrine and Covenants by reading the Book of Mormon or the Bible. I think we have to read and study the Doctrine and Covenants, pray over it, and live the principles that are there. As we live them and experience them, then we get a testimony of them. I don't believe we get a testimony of the Word of Wisdom unless we really live the Word of Wisdom. I don't think we get a testimony of the divine calling of the President of the Church until we have had experience which will give us that testimony.

We could go down through the whole list of principles. I believe that if I am going to get a testimony of any one of them, I have got to study it, pray over it, and then live it. Then by living it and experiencing it, I get the testimony. The composite of all of the testimonies pertaining to these various principles all together give to me a testimony of the gospel as a whole. That is the way I understand it. (*Mark E. Petersen*, UA-CHD, 11 July 1956 — Provo, Utah, p. 13.)

(4D-7) *A knowledge of God does not come instantaneously.* Generally, you will not gain a knowledge of the things of God on an instantaneous basis. The dimension of time is an inseparable factor in the strengthening and building of spiritual things into your life. You are a generation that is, I think, up against this instantaneous culture as Dr. Silber puts it. You will leave here today, and you will have an instantaneous lunch, you will go to an instantaneous class, and you might turn on some instantaneous music. Maybe you will have a multimedia experience in which you go someplace and three or four cameras bombard you at the same time without any regard for what you can really absorb, think through, and understand.

We see this in the Church sometimes. Young missionaries often become sullen and unhappy, feeling that they have failed because they have not instantly become missionaries after being in the language training mission or in the mission field for just a few days. They do not realize that these elements have to be acquired and developed, that they come by doing the right thing over a period of time. These elements involve the passing of time and using time wisely and effectively.

The Brethren have people who come to them for instantaneous advice. Sometimes they get letters from people, asking, "In a paragraph or two, please tell me what your secret of success is so that I can apply it in the shortest possible time and become a success too." In looking at the life of a President Smith or a President Lee or a President Tanner, we see nothing instantaneous. Their success is the application of principles of truth and righteousness over a lifetime, day in and day out — offering the prayers, having the faith, meeting the trials. It is a gradual process, and it requires not only the application of the principles of truth and righteousness but also the passage of time.

Some people look for instantaneous answers to prayers and become dejected and have their faith shaken because they make an instant prayer and the Lord does not give an instant answer. They do not understand that in the process of life and in the passage of time the Lord answers just about all our prayers, but many times the answers are unfolded to us as time goes on. The answer does not always come when the question is raised. But again, it is part of this process of time.

Finally, some people believe in instantaneous repentance. While you can stop doing something instantaneously and get back on the right track instantaneously, true repentance occurs when you have demonstrated, through the passage of time, that what you resolved to do has actually come to pass and is truly out of your life.

We are taught that even the Savior, when he lived upon the earth, had to grow from grace to grace until such time as he overcame all things. We must realize that a knowledge of what we have been speaking of — the message of the restoration — will not come through what Dr. Silber refers to as the instant culture or maybe the pollution of time. In order to gain this knowledge we have to build things into our lives as we live those lives, and time itself will begin to help us if we are following the right principles and teachings. We will gradually receive the knowledge, testimony, and understanding of the things we seek. This is not an instant process. It is the purpose of our whole mortal probation. It is an ongoing thing. (*Loren C. Dunn*, BYU, 7 Mar. 1972, pp. 3-4.)

5

BECOMING
INDEPENDENT
WITNESSES

A.   The Requirement to Know for Ourselves

(5A-1) *Superficial knowledge.* I fear that too many Latter-day Saints know the Gospel only superficially, and take most of it for granted, without making the effort of inquiry. This is in direct contradiction to the Gospel principle that every member of the Church, must, as it were, stand upon his own feet, and know for himself that the Gospel is true. (*John A. Widtsoe*, CR, Apr. 1939, p. 22.)

(5A-2) *A testimony so strong that when mortals fall you do not.* From my boyhood I have desired to learn the principles of the gospel in such a way and to such an extent that it would matter not to me who might fall from the truth, who might make a mistake, who might fail to continue to follow the example of the Master, my foundation would be sure and certain in the truths that I have learned though all men else go astray and fail of obedience to them. We all have heard of people who have pinned their faith to the arm of flesh, who have felt that their belief, their confidence and their love for the principles of the gospel of Jesus Christ would be shattered if their ideals — those possibly who first taught them the principles of the Gospel — should make a mistake, falter or fall.

I know of but one in all the world who can be taken as the first and only perfect standard for us to follow, and He is the Only Begotten Son of God. (*Joseph F. Smith, JI, Nov. 1916, pp. 738-739.*)

(5A-3) *It could be a bad thing for us to depend on others.* I would hate to think that there are many of us . . . that tied our testimonies to what other people said. It would be a bad thing for us to depend for our testimonies upon what some man said, however great or however small he might be.

I remember years ago having read somewhere, as I recall, a testimonial that Napoleon wrote regarding God or regarding the Savior, I do not remember which. But you know, it does not make a bit of difference to me what Napoleon thought about either God or the Savior, so far as my belief is concerned. My testimony is what I think and what I get here in my heart. That is the thing that counts with you, that counts with me.

They tell a story of a Dutch judge that might illustrate the position in which anyone would be who pinned his faith on the testimony of others. This judge had before him a man on trial for murder. The prosecution produced six witnesses who saw the man commit the murder. The defense produced six witnesses who did not see the man commit the murder [laughter] and the man went free.

Now I am thinking about someone collecting a half-dozen men who could testify to him of God's goodness and mercy and love, and then finding another half-dozen who could not testify that they had any blessings that the others had. Would the investigation conclude there was no God?

My point is, get your own testimony. (*J. Reuben Clark, Jr.*, BYU, 27 May 1958, p. 4.)

(5A-4) *To know for ourselves, independent of others.* But what I desire to point attention to . . . is the fact that revelation is not restricted to the prophet of God on earth. The visions of eternity are not reserved for apostles — they are not reserved for General Authorities. Revelation is something that should be received by every individual. God is no respecter of persons, and every soul, in the ultimate sense, is just as precious in His sight as the souls of those that are called to positions of leadership. Because He operates on principles of eternal, universal and never-deviating law, any individual that abides the law which entitles him to get revelation can know exactly and precisely what . . . [the President of the Church] . . . knows, can entertain angels just as well as Joseph Smith entertained them, and can be in tune in full measure with all of the things of the Spirit.

Now for a text I read to you these words of the Prophet Joseph Smith. He said: "Reading the experience of others, or the revelations given to *them*, can never give *us* a comprehensive view of our condition and true relation to God. Knowledge of these things can only be obtained by experience through the ordinances of God set forth for that purpose. Could you gaze into heaven five minutes, you would know more than you would by reading all that ever was written on the subject." (*Teachings of the Prophet Joseph Smith,* page 324.)

Now note this statement: "Could you gaze into heaven five minutes, you would know more than you would by reading all that ever was written on the subject." I think our concern is to get personal revelation, to know for ourselves, independent of any other individual or set of individuals, what the mind and the will of the Lord is as pertaining to his Church and as pertaining to us in our individual concerns. (*Bruce R. McConkie,* BYU, 11 Oct. 1966, pp. 2-3.)

(5A-5) *Standing upon our own two feet, spiritually speaking.* I have been interested in a quotation that I picked up from Heber C. Kimball. Speaking in terms of having a partial testimony, being able to stand and say, "I believe the Church is true, hoping that some day I might be able to stand and say, 'I know the Church is true,' " Brother Kimball had this to say:

> The Church has before it many close places through which it will have to pass before the work of God is crowned with victory. To meet the difficulties that are coming, it will be necessary for you to have a knowledge of the truth of this work for yourselves. The difficulties will be of such a character that the man or woman who does not possess this personal knowledge or witness, will fall. If you [do not have a] testimony, *live right* and call upon the Lord, and cease not until you obtain it. If you do not, you will not stand. . . . The time will come when no man or woman will be able to stand on borrowed light. Each of you will have to be guided with the light within himself. If you

do not have it, how can you stand? (Whitney, *Life of Heber C. Kimball*, pages 449-450. Italics added.)

So, my wonderful young friends, how important it is that we learn to stand upon our own two feet, spiritually speaking. Many of us cling to the testimony of a good bishop, a quorum leader, an MIA leader, or our parents, without going through the motions that are necessary to one day bring *us* the light and knowledge we must have that we might be able to stand in the last days. (*Robert L. Simpson*, BYU, 18 Oct. 1966, pp. 7-8.)

(5A-6) *That person has not lived up to his or her requirements.* It is a requirement the Lord makes of every member of the Church that he know for himself and have a testimony of the truth in his own heart and not be under the necessity of depending upon anyone else to know that Jesus Christ is the Son of God or that Joseph Smith is a prophet of God. If there is any person in the sound of my voice, a member of this Church, who does not know in his heart that the Father and the Son appeared to Joseph Smith, revealed themselves, and made known again the true doctrine concerning God, then that person has not lived up to his or her requirements, the commandments the Lord has placed upon us, for we should know that fact. We should know that John the Baptist came and restored the Aaronic Priesthood. We ought not to have to depend upon any other source, only the light of truth which is planted in our hearts by the Holy Spirit through our faithfulness. We should know that Peter, James, and John came and restored the Melchizedek Priesthood with all its powers, so that the gospel again could be preached, the knowledge of God declared, and righteousness again be found in the earth, for the salvation of all those who would repent of their sins and turn unto God. (*Joseph Fielding Smith*, CR, Oct. 1952, p. 60.)

(5A-7) *We need to mature beyond that point.* We do right for various reasons. Some people do right simply because they don't want to be punished for doing wrong. When we do right for fear of retribution, I think our foundation is very shaky. Another might say, "I want to do right because I have always been taught that this is the thing to do." Well, such reasoning is based on hearsay, on the testimony of others, and I think we need to mature beyond that point. I think we need to have our own testimonies, instead of the advice of others on a perpetual basis. Others have been heard to say, "I want to do right just to please my parents," and although we all should have a desire to please our parents, that reason alone is not sufficient to sustain us throughout eternity. Perhaps you have heard people who have indicated that they are doing the right thing simply because they want to be obedient to God's commandments; this, too, is a very high and noble purpose — provided, of course, that the obedience is not blind obedience, without personal conviction. But to me the best reason of all is illustrated by the person who feels the desire to do right because he wants to add glory to his Father in heaven. Whatever stage of motivation we find ourselves in, I think we must eventually reinforce this with our own personal testimony which has been built on a foundation of gospel scholarship and understanding — a testimony which leads us to the life of unselfish-ness and service, one which finds its highest sanctification in the supreme thought that we are living gospel principles because we desire to glorify his great name. (*Robert L. Simpson*, BYU, 1974, pp. 55-56.)

(5A-8) *A testimony of temporal as well as spiritual things.* In giving instructions to the people, the authorities of the Church have fre-quently advised that the members should know the truth for them-selves. "Every man must know for himself and not for another." "Stand on your own foundation." "Have a testimony for yourself." These sentences, and many of similar import, have well nigh become platitudes, they have been used so often by the authorities in their exhortations to the people. But these instructions have had their effect upon the Latter-day Saints, and to such an extent that it is no exaggera-tion to say that no other community is so well informed individually upon the doctrines of the Gospel as the Latter-day Saints. Let a member make an error in teaching, and he will find any number of his listeners who will interpose objections and offer corrections. Study, individual testimony, the light of the Spirit of God, have combined to give the average member of the Church such a keen knowledge of the truth, that no person can deceive him; and, further, no member will hesitate a moment but, if occasion offers, will freely declare his knowledge. This has made the people independent, confident, content, steadfast in the midst of whirlwinds of diversified doctrines, theological contentions, and cries of lo here, and lo there, is the Christ! They are not carried about by every wind of doctrine, "by the sleight of men, and cunning craftiness, whereby they lie in wait to deceive." They have come to a "unity of the faith and of the knowledge of the Son of God." In the midst of it all, they go about their duty, immovable, firm in the knowledge of truth.

And how has this come about? By study, by testimony gained by the inspiration of the Holy Ghost, by proving the doctrine in personal practice, and holding fast the good. They have thus a perfect personal knowledge; if it were not so, the Church organization could not hold together, "but now the whole body is safely joined together." If members did not know for themselves that the work is of God, and that its doctrines are true, the organization would crumble to pieces in a short time. But do the statements of sensational newspapers affect the faith of the Latter-day Saints? Do they begin to doubt when ministers or laymen attack the principles of the Gospel? Not at all! Provided what is said is confined to faith, repentance, baptism for the living and the dead, organization of the Church with apostles and prophets, and to other doctrines pertaining to spiritual salvation and exaltation; but it will be seen that to the temporal affairs, and matters pertaining to the immediate government of the Church, this statement does not in all cases apply. But a little thought will convince any one that the latter is quite as essential as the former, for without the temporal, there can be no expression of the spiritual.

Long ago it was discovered, by the opposition to the work of God, that attacking the Latter-day Saints on the principles of the Gospel was of little or no avail. They have even long ago abandoned their attacks on the Book of Mormon, and instead tolerate, even actually adopt, many of its doctrines.

But new tactics are now chosen, and these on the line of temporal affairs. Everything now done by the Church officers in a temporal way, they proclaim, is done to the detriment of the people, who are being robbed, plundered, impoverished and distressed. The leaders are enriching themselves at the expense of the Saints, and the Church has become a vast commercial combination, having for its object the distress and financial destruction of the people. Tithing is a robbery, they would have us believe, designed to keep the members in bondage and subjection, and to enrich the leaders, who are revelling in wealth and luxury.

Strange to say, there are a few of the Saints who pay attention to these charges. Why to these attacks, and not to those of doctrine? It must be because the Saints are not so well informed on the lives and actions of their leaders, and on the temporal affairs of the Church, as upon the doctrines and the spiritual things. It must be because they do not know the truth for themselves. They do not stand on their own foundation. They have not a testimony for themselves. They are not informed individually. It is for these reasons that they fear the attacks of newspaper writers and others who lie for personal, political or mercenary motives; or, if they do not lie, so cunningly mix truth and error that there is a plausible appearance to their conclusions. They knowingly twist and misconstrue every word and action of the authorities. Statements, activities, movements, innocent in themselves, are, by misconstruction and misapplication, and for sinister effect upon the unknowing, made to appear as colossal lies, damnable dealings, treacherous incidents, tending towards immorality, rottenness and evil.

All this should have no effect upon the Latter-day Saint except to cause him to determine that he will know for himself. If he so knows, he will take no misrepresentation for granted. When he has investigated and learned for himself, he will be as immovable in these things as he now is in affairs of doctrine. The liars and defamers will be laid bare before his view, and to the eye of his understanding their mercenary motives will be made plain. (*Joseph F. Smith*, IE, Aug. 1905, pp. 773-775.)

(5A-9) *They do not dig down to the root of things.* I realize that there is indifference to some extent among the Latter-day Saints. I have thought sometimes that they have felt it was not necessary for them to seek an individual testimony of the truth of this work. They have satisfied themselves with the knowledge which their parents possessed of the divinity of the Gospel and the prophetic power which God conferred upon Joseph Smith. They are willing to listen to the counsels of the authorities of the Church and accept the theories which are advanced concerning our religion; but they do not seem disposed, for some reason, to seek for a practical and an undying testimony of the truth of this Gospel, without which no man or woman is sure of eternal life. They doubtless attend meetings because in this day it is fashionable to attend church; it is fashionable to study theology and to read the scriptures not seeking therein the inspiration which the scriptures contain, but reading them because it is considered an excellent literary work. In this spirit many of the young people read it. They read the works of the Church because of the historical information therein to be obtained. But they do not dig down to the root of things, to gain for themselves a testimony of the truth. (*Abraham H. Cannon*, DW, 16 June 1894, p. 801.)

(5A-10) *No man should trust solely the testimony of another.* It is some-times taught among us that we should follow Brother Joseph or Brother Brigham, or some other leader, and do as they say, and that is all that is required. Now this is in one sense a false doctrine. No man should trust solely the testimony of another. He should have a direct testimony from God for himself. Then obedience is intelligent and not blind. I might have listened to Joseph Smith testify to the truth of the Book of Mormon until I was old as Methuselah, and in the end I would have gone away in darkness had I not received a testimony from God that he was a prophet and that he knew by revelation whereof he spoke. (*Brigham Young*, WW, pp. 377-378.)

(5A-11) *Too much confidence in the testimonies of others.* The other day one of the bishops . . . came to my office, and told me that frequently there came to their conferences visiting brethren who talked about those who criticize the General Authorities of the Church, and about the "isms" that are springing up in apostate groups. He said, "You know, Brother Lee, our people don't know what these brethren are talking about up there in our ward. We never hear these criticisms. They accept you brethren as the representatives of the Living God, and we don't hear what they say is happening elsewhere."

As I thought of that bishop's statement, I remembered the words of Brigham Young:

> Were your faith concentrated upon the proper object, your confidence unshaken, your lives pure and holy, every one fulfilling the duty of his or her calling according to the priest-hood and capacity bestowed upon you, you would be filled with the Holy Ghost, and it would be as impossible for any man to deceive and to lead you to destruction as for a feather to remain unconsumed in the midst of intense heat.

And then this:

I am more afraid that this people have so much confidence in their leaders that they will not inquire for themselves of God whether they are being led by him. I am fearful they settle down in a state of blind security, trusting their eternal destiny in the hands of their leaders with a reckless confidence that in itself would thwart the purposes of God in their salvation, and weaken that influence they could give their leaders if they know for themselves by the revelations of Jesus Christ that they are led in the right way. Let every man and woman know by the whisperings of the Spirit of God to themselves whether their leaders are walking in the way the Lord dictates or not.

To me, there is a tremendous truth. It is not alone sufficient for us as Latter-day Saints to follow our leaders and to accept their counsel, but we have the greater obligation to gain for ourselves the unshakable testimony of the divine appointment of these men and the witness that what they have told us is the will of our Heavenly Father. (*Harold B. Lee*, CR, Oct. 1950, p. 130.)

(5A-12) *A fault to be avoided: living on borrowed light.* One fault to be avoided by the Saints, young and old, is the tendency to live on borrowed light, with their own hidden under a bushel; to permit the savor of their salt of knowledge to be lost; and the light within them to be reflected rather than original.

Such a condition is wrong. Every Saint should not only have the light within himself, through the inspiration of the Holy Spirit, but his light should so shine that it may be clearly perceived by others. Then they will not be in the very awkward and perilous position of some who are drawn hither and thither, as the clouds come and go over men from whom they borrow their light. This class of people, so driven, do not depend upon their own knowledge or judgment, or testimony, but are ever dependent upon the opinions of others. They believe this or that, passing from one belief to another, as some one else believes or disbe-lieves. They are always in a stew, fretting over matters religious, political and social, which men of firm convictions and self-possession count as of little or no import. They walk in borrowed light; in darkness, they are without initiative; and when clouds obscure their source of light, they lose the way. (*Joseph F. Smith*, IE, Nov. 1904, p. 61.)

(5A-13) *Statements of others should be confirmed by the spirit.* While all members of the Church should respect, support, and heed the teachings of the Authorities of the Church, no one should accept a statement and base his testimony upon it, no matter who makes it, until he has, under mature examination, found it to be true and worthwhile; then his logical deductions may be confirmed by the spirit of revelation to his spirit because real conversion must come from within. (*Hugh B. Brown*, RS, Oct. 1969, p. 724.)

B.   The Necessity for Standing Independent

(5B-1) *The time is here to stand on your own feet.* I would pray that you could feel the love flowing from my soul to yours, and know of my deep compassion toward each of you as you face the problems of today. The time is here when each of you must stand on your own feet. Be converted, because no one can endure on borrowed light. You will have to be guided by the light within yourself. If you do not have it, you will not stand. (*Harold B. Lee*, NE, Feb. 1971, p. 4.)

(5B-2) *Withstanding the tide of trouble.* Every man has got to learn to stand upon his own knowledge; he cannot depend upon his neighbor; every man must be independent; he must depend upon his God for himself entirely. It depends upon himself to see if he will stand the tide of trouble and overcome the impediments that are strewed in the pathway of life to prevent his progress. (*Lorenzo Snow*, MS, 10 Dec. 1888, p. 806.)

(5B-3) *To be prepared for the millennial reign.* Each member of the Church, to be prepared for the millennial reign, must receive a testimony, each for himself, of the divinity of the work established by Joseph Smith. It was this that was taught plainly by the Saints after the advent of the Savior upon the earth, and one of the leaders in our day has said it again, when he declared, I suppose with reference to the parable of the five foolish and five wise virgins in the Master's parable, "The time will come when no man or woman will be able to endure on borrowed light. Each will have to be guided by the light within himself." (*Life of Heber C. Kimball*, pp. 449-450.) (*Harold B. Lee*, CR, Oct. 1956, p. 62.)

(5B-4) *No man should be satisfied until he has secured a perfect assurance.*
No man should be satisfied until he has secured a perfect assurance that
this is the path of exaltation and glory; that Joseph Smith was a prophet
of God; that these things which I have been reading to you are actually
of God; that Jesus, the Son of God, actually appeared in 1836 to some of
the sons and daughters of God that were acquainted with Him in the
other life. There is no question about this in my mind, and there are
tens of thousands of Latter-day Saints that can testify to the truth of this
work. They know it for themselves; but I fear there are too many that
have not secured that assurance that is absolutely necessary, because
every man and every woman will be tried to see how far he or she has an
understanding in regard to these principles. (*Lorenzo Snow*, DW, 1 June
1895, p. 738.)

(5B-5) *And who will be able to stand?* Latter-day Saints, you must think
for yourselves. No man or woman can remain in this Church on
borrowed light. I am a strong believer in the following statement made
by my father in the House of the Lord [Endowment House] in 1856.

> We think we are secure in the chambers of the everlasting hills,
> but the time will come when we will be so mixed up that it will
> be difficult to tell the face of a Saint from the face of an enemy
> to the people of God. Then, brethren, look out for the great
> sieve, for there will be a great sifting time, and many will fall;
> for I say unto you there is a test, a test, a TEST coming, and who
> will be able to stand?

(*J. Golden Kimball*, CR, Apr. 1904, pp. 28-29.)

(5B-6) *The only thing that will keep you in the Church.* The only thing that
will keep you in this Church (Oh, we have many members, don't forget
that, but many of them will never be in the Church when the time of
testing comes) is a faith, which cannot be shaken, in the Lord Jesus
Christ and his work, which makes your love for him real. (*S. Dilworth
Young*, BYU, 1 July 1969, p. 12.)

(5B-7) *A testimony strong enough to withstand the test.* My mother has told
me that the last time father [Heber C. Kimball] took a walk down Main
Street, after he was stricken with paralysis, he returned with difficulty
back to his home, the residence which still stands on the hill, and he
said to her, "OH THE TEST, THE TEST, THE TEST, who will be able

to stand?" Mother said, "What is the test?" He replied, "I don't know, but it is only those that know that Jesus is the Christ that can stand." . . .

If the Latter-day Saints do not know that Jesus is the Christ, and that this is His Church, I tell you, in the name of the Lord, you will not stand, you will be among the number that will fall. (*J. Golden Kimball,* CR, Apr. 1906, p. 77.)

(5B-8) *We will be tried to the very core.* How many are there among this people who, if drawn to the line and the plummet, could stand up and say they were filled with the Spirit of God, and that they did actually know for themselves that they were living up to their religion, that they knew Joseph Smith was an inspired prophet, and that they knew this to be the great work of God? I hope all who have assembled here to-day are able to bear this humble testimony; and should there be any who cannot do this, I conjure them to rest not until they can say so, for the day is coming when we will be put to the test — when we will be tried to the very core. We will all see the day, when you will find these words to be true. You must know that Jesus is the Christ, that "Mormonism" is true, or you will not stand and endure to the end. Why is it, then, that so many of the Saints are negligent, and disgrace the priesthood which they bear? (*Orson F. Whitney,* MS, 7 Jan 1889, p. 2.)

(5B-9) *Deep-rooted conviction necessary for the trials.* Could anything that might occur to you, or that might take place in the Church, or with her officers or authorities, change your faith in the purposes, and in the absolute justice and mercy, of the Lord, or in the saving power of his gospel, the message of his salvation? If so, your faith is not deep-rooted, and there is strong need of your becoming convinced. . . .

Unless the Saints have an actual knowledge that the course which they are pursuing is in harmony with the will of God, they will grow weary in trial, and will faint under persecution and contumely. But, on the contrary, with this trust in God burned into their souls, no matter what comes, they are happy in doing his will, knowing full well that at last the promise shall be theirs. Thus is the world overcome, and the crown of glory obtained which God has laid away for those who love, honor and obey him. (*Joseph F. Smith,* IE, Nov. 1903, pp. 53, 55.)

(5B-10) *Help in time of trials.* How frequently we have been urged . . . to secure for ourselves a testimony of the truth of the gospel! Whenever a time of trial comes, if we live our religion we have that testimony and nothing can move us. We have been taught from the beginning that every individual member in the Church must have the unwavering witness of the Holy Ghost, or he will not endure to the end. So many have passed along, lived and died as Saints, without meeting those serious trials, it is quite possible some may have concluded that such an injunction was born of enthusiasm, and that we can go through with all our religious experiences without any witness superior to our own good sense and native judgment. We can embrace no greater fallacy. The witness of the Holy Ghost is indispensably necessary to the successful life of every individual Saint. Wherein we have not been tried, there is nothing more certain than that we will be. (*Francis M. Lyman*, JI, 1 Jan. 1887, p. 3.)

6

"FEELINGS" ARE ASSOCIATED WITH A TESTIMONY

A.   A Testimony Can Be "Felt"

(6A-1) *He cannot measure, weigh or count it.* He who has a testimony does not know exactly of what it is made, or where it came from. He cannot measure it. He cannot weigh it. He cannot count it. He can only feel it. That is the testimony and it is like a breeze or the dew. We were in Upper Galilee the other day, and there you have the dews of heaven that the Lord talked about. Even though there had been no clouds in the sky, there were a million little sparkling diamonds on the little blades of grass. This early, it was very wet. When did the dew fall? Nobody saw it fall. Nobody knew when it came. It was just there all at once. When did it come? When was the grass wet?

It is a warm day. You stand perspiring in the warmth and all at once there is a little cooling wind or breeze. You feel it — a pleasant cooling sensation. You do not know from where it comes, but all at once you are cooled and refreshed and that is like the Spirit when a man is born again. (*Spencer W. Kimball,* UA-CHD, 15 Jan. 1962 — Berlin, Germany, pp. 3-4.)

(6A-2) *I can feel just as good as anybody else.* I am reminded of an experience that happened in the life of President George Albert Smith. Several years before he became President of the Church, he gave a home for some months to a couple from Holland. They could speak but a few words of English and could understand very little English. However, the Dutch brother insisted on going to the English-speaking fast meetings and after about the third fast meeting as President Smith and he were walking back to the Smith home, President Smith asked, "Why is it that you insist on going to the English-speaking fast meeting when you understand so little of what is being said?" Here was the significant reply from the Dutch brother, "It is not what I see that makes me happy. It is not what I hear that makes me happy. It is what I feel that makes me happy, and I can feel just as good as anybody."

Yes, there are many who hear and yet do not hear. There are many who see, yet do not see. If our lives are in tune with the glorious teachings of the gospel of Jesus Christ, then we can feel just as good as anybody. We feel as good as anybody because we have a witness and a conviction that Jesus is the Christ. (*John Longden,* CR, Oct. 1958, pp. 68-69.)

(6A-3) *On rare and marvelous occasions.* In order to gain a thorough understanding of what it means to have the Holy Ghost bear witness to one's heart, a person must have that experience. One who has done so knows that the power of the Holy Ghost may come to an individual in varying degrees. On most occasions it bears witness to one quite gently, but there may be a few occasions in one's life when that divine power enters his body with such overwhelming force that he feels as if it might consume his flesh, such as was experienced by the ancient apostles on the day of Pentecost and by Heber C. Kimball at his baptism and confirmation. Brother Kimball wrote: ". . . I received the Holy Ghost, as the disciples did in ancient days, which was like consuming fire. . . . it seemed as though my body would consume away." (*Life of Heber C. Kimball,* 1945 ed., p. 22.)

On these rare and marvelous occasions, one feels the power of the Holy Ghost enter his body as if it were a wave of electricity. While he is under that spiritual influence, he experiences an indescribable joy throughout his whole being. Yes, he feels a love for everybody and everything far surpassing his natural ability to feel love and joy on other occasions. An experience of this kind is more dynamic, more powerful, and more awe-inspiring than any sensation that could be received through the physical senses. Such a dynamic experience leaves a lasting impression on the recipient that time does not dim and that he can never deny. (*Milton R. Hunter,* CR, Oct. 1965, pp. 82-83.)

(6A-4) *I have felt that thrill.* I am telling you plainly and frankly that the greatest joy, the greatest peace, and the greatest happiness I have ever had in my life have come when speaking under the spirit of testimony. I have felt that thrill throughout my being. It is a joy and happiness that cannot be expressed. (*J. Golden Kimball,* CR, Oct. 1935, p. 35.)

(6A-5) *"You shall feel that it is right."* In modern revelation the Lord has established a spiritual test to find truth.

He says in the ninth section of the Doctrine and Covenants simply: "But behold, I say unto you, that you must study it out in your mind; then you must ask me if it be right, and if it is right I will cause that your bosom shall burn within you; therefore, you shall feel that it is right." (V. 8.)

The words "you shall feel that it is right" refer to a feeling of peace and warmth, a feeling that touches the soul. For an investigator of the truth, this feeling begins to come when the missionaries come and leave their message. They can feel it in the home after the missionaries leave. They can feel it in the congregations of the Saints; and they can feel it as they read and study and pray about the message. It is a feeling that is unique in its peace and joy because it emanates from Jesus Christ. It is that feeling which brings a greater knowledge and a more sure witness than even flesh and bones. (*Loren C. Dunn,* CR, Apr. 1977, p. 43.)

(6A-6) *I feel it in my soul – my whole being.* Now, my brethren and sisters, I know that my Redeemer lives, I feel it in every fiber of my being. I am just as satisfied of it as I am of my own existence. I cannot feel more sure of my own being than I do that my Redeemer lives, and that my God lives, the Father of my Savior. I feel it in my soul; I am converted to it in my whole being. (*Joseph F. Smith,* MS, 19 Feb. 1903, pp. 118-119.)

(6A-7) *He has made me to feel it.* The Lord Jesus Christ said, and it was one of the first principles laid down in the book of Doctrine and Covenants, that if we would do the will of the Father we would *know* of the doctrine that it was of God. Now, Joseph Smith laid down that doctrine the same as Jesus did, and there is a test by which men may know that the Gospel is true. It is the privilege of every man to know that it is the truth. Now, then, comes the final great test. Who shall say to me, "You do not know that the testimonies of these men are true. You believe it." Certainly I do; I believe it with all my soul. "But how do you know?" . . . It is hard to define to you that do not know; it is hard to explain to outsiders how I know the truth of these things; but I say to you in all sincerity and honesty of heart that I know that this work is true, because the Lord Almighty, through the power of His Spirit and its impressions upon my soul, has made me to feel it from the crown of my head to the soles of my feet. God has shown it to me and removed all doubt from my mind, and I accept it as I accept the fact that the sun shines at mid-day. (*Joseph F. Smith*, MS, 4 Oct. 1906, p. 628.)

B.   Learning to Interpret the "Spirit"

(6B-1) *The greatest, most thrilling, most joyful earthly experience.* Some of you may have had great adventures in the hills, and some of you may have had them on the water and the sea, some have had them or will have them in the air, but I can testify to you that there will be none of you have any adventure greater, more thrilling, and more joyful than finding out how to interpret the Spirit which comes into you bearing testimony of the truth. Young folks have to learn how, so do we older folks. We have to find out the technique by which the Spirit whispers in our hearts. We have to learn to hear it and to understand it and to know when we have it, and that sometimes takes a long time.

But no matter what your age, you do not need to wait until you are old to know. Any child, age eight, having been baptized and having received the gift of the Holy Ghost, is a fit candidate to have the Holy Ghost bear its imprint upon him as to the truth of the teachings of the Church of Jesus Christ of Latter-day Saints. As he grows and has that imprint upon him, he will have joy and satisfaction and peace and happiness beyond anything that can be described with words.

So I would say to the young folks of the Church, some of whom come to me confused, if you will ask, not doubting that you can have an answer, the answer will come in the whispering. Then you must learn to interpret the whispering. At first it likely will come as something akin to a feeling, although not a feeling. There will finally come into your minds the words expressive of the feeling, and those words properly interpreted will be the whispering of the Spirit. (*S. Dilworth Young*, CR, Apr. 1959, p. 59.)

(6B-2) *Each of us is a Helen Keller in one way.* Each of us is a Helen Keller in one way. You see, when you were eight years of age (about the time that Miss Sullivan came into the life of Helen Keller) you were given . . . the Holy Ghost. I would suspect that that great spirit has about as hard a time reaching us with his influence as Miss Sullivan had teaching Miss Keller. As I look back over my life I realize the numbers of times that I am sure the spirit of the Holy Ghost has tried to teach me what I should know, and be, and do, and where I was going. I am dismayed at the number of times that even though the influence was there, I did not recognize it, could not feel it, could not understand it. . . . The spirit you were given on your admission to the Church has a commission to teach you all truth, to lead you back into the presence of God through his influence, through his whispering. You would do well to learn to hear the whispering. . . . But my guess is that, like me, you are going to have about as tough a time learning as Miss Keller had. (S. Dilworth Young, BYU, 28 Oct. 1959, pp. 4-5.)

(6B-3) *The spirit is more anxious to help us than we are anxious to be helped.* I have discovered that one is guided sometimes even if he does not ask for it. Nearly all of the occasions in my life when I have had great events foretold me by the Spirit, I have never invited them myself or asked about them. They have just come. I can see why that is: because every person who joins the Church and is a member of it in good standing has a right to receive the constant companionship of the Holy Ghost. He is given the right at baptism and he keeps that right as long as he is righteous. I have come to the conclusion that this Spirit and whatever influence he uses to reach us is more anxious to help us than we are anxious to be helped. . . . So you may be sure that if you are doing your normal things in righteousness, there will come to you intuitions, feelings, revelations which will guide you if you can understand that Spirit and how you're having it. It takes a little work to understand when it is there, but you can learn it. (S. Dilworth Young, BYU, 1977, p. 96.)

C. Susceptibility to the Spirit

(6C-1) *Some blood strains are more susceptible.* It seems to me, however, that there runs in some blood strains a higher susceptibility to the refining and saving influence of testimony than in other strains. I don't know that I understand it, but I have thought that the significance of the "blood of Israel" is that there is in that great blood strain, following the blessings and promises of God, a susceptibility to the influence of the Holy Spirit, that does not run in other strains. . . . I believe that testimony runs in the blood. I believe that it is inheritable, and that the tendency to faith may descend from father to son. It seems to me that Paul had that in mind when, writing to Timothy, he said in substance: "I do perceive in thee the faith that was in thy grandmother Lois," thus recognizing that this tendency to faith, this susceptibility to testimony, courses along in the very blood strains of the race. (*Stephen L Richards,* CR, Oct. 1925, pp. 118-119.)

(6C-2) *Those who developed the talent for spirituality.* Our elders go out and teach, and some people have a warm, calm assurance that what they have said is true, and other people don't. This is exactly what is intended. The whole system is to determine who gets a warm comforting assurance when the testimony is borne and who does not. The people who believe the testimonies easily are those who developed in the preexistence the talent for spirituality. If we developed that talent back there, then we are born with it here and it is easier for us to believe than it is for somebody else. Our article of faith says, quite properly, that "all mankind may be saved, by obedience to the laws and ordinances of the Gospel." (Third Article of Faith.) But it is easier for some people to believe than others. (*Bruce R. McConkie,* ACR, Feb. 1976 — Sydney, Australia, p. 21.)

7

THE ROLE
OF INTELLECT
AND REASON

A.   Intellect Is Not Enough

(7A-1) *A mental conviction is only preparatory.* The first great revelation that anyone receives is called a testimony of the Gospel. A testimony presupposes revelation. You may study the Gospel at extended length and come up with the conclusion, from a mental standpoint, that it is true, but if that is all that is involved, you do not have a testimony. That may be helpful; that may get you thinking in the right field and analyzing in the right direction; it may cause you to try to do the things that will cause the Holy Ghost to speak to you and give you a testimony. Reason is not to be downgraded. We should use all the reason and judgment and sense and wisdom that we can get. But it is just preparatory; it just opens the door and the final testimony comes *only* from the Holy Ghost. And when the Holy Spirit speaks, then we know with absolute certainty. We say we have a testimony. (*Bruce R. McConkie,* UU, 22 Jan. 1971, p. 5.)

(7A-2) *You must go to the spiritual laboratory.* Why, oh, why do people think they can fathom the most complex spiritual depths without the necessary experimental and laboratory work accompanied by compliance with the laws that govern it? Absurd it is, but you will frequently find popular personalities, who seem never to have lived a single law of

God, discoursing in interviews on religion. How ridiculous for such persons to attempt to outline for the world a way of life!

And yet many a financier, politician, college professor, or owner of a gambling club thinks that because he has risen above all his fellowmen in his particular field he knows everything in every field. One cannot know God nor understand his works or plans unless he follows the laws which govern. The spiritual realm, which is just as absolute as is the physical, cannot be understood by the laws of the physical. You do not learn to make electric generators in a seminary. Neither do you learn certain truths about spiritual things in a physics laboratory. You must go to the spiritual laboratory, use the facilities available there, and comply with the governing rules. Then you may know these truths just as surely, or more surely, than the scientist knows the metals, or the acids, or other elements. (*Spencer W. Kimball*, BYU, 1977, p. 139.)

(7A-3) *The limitations of earthly philosophies.* Man, by philosophy and the exercise of his natural intelligence, may gain an understanding, to some extent, of the laws of Nature. But to comprehend God, heavenly wisdom and intelligence are necessary. Earthly and heavenly philosophy are two different things, and it is folly for men to base their arguments upon earthly philosophy in trying to unravel the mysteries of the kingdom of God. (*John Taylor*, DW, 30 Mar. 1870, p. 92.)

(7A-4) *When the light rested upon me I saw* . . . In Joseph Smith's story are two lines I call to your attention and invite you to consider. You know the story — the search, the darkness that almost overcame the boy, and then a line that says, "*When the light rested upon me I saw. . . .*" We customarily do not stop where I have just stopped. What he says is, "*When the light rested upon me I saw . . .*" and then tells what he saw and what they did. Think of the first words, "*When the light rested upon me . . .*" When the light came, when I had the light, I could see. A few lines later he says, "*When the light had departed I had no strength.*" Perhaps you haven't read it that way. Maybe you will from now on if you haven't because the message is the same as section 50 of the Doctrine and Covenants. What are you called to? What are you ordained to? Why do you preach the gospel? And how? "*Through my Spirit.*" If you do it through my Spirit it is of me. If you don't, if you try to do it some other way, however well educated and bright you are, then it isn't of me. And if you try to learn my word in any other way than through that Spirit, then that isn't of me either. That may be the most sobering single lesson I now know in connection with what I know about the Lord and the love I have for Him. (*Marion D. Hanks*, UU, 12 May 1978, pp. 5-6.)

(7A-5) *Anything a person can be reasoned into, he can be reasoned out of.* There are many people today who attempt to gain a testimony of truth in their own way, or, perhaps better said, by the methods and power of man. In other words, they attempt to gain a testimony by the power of reason. They forget that anything a person can be reasoned into, he can be reasoned out of. An intellectual testimony is no stronger than the intellect that possesses it. Another person with a greater intellect can come along and by his superior reasoning power he can rob that person of his testimony. When, however, a testimony is obtained by the power of the Spirit and testified to by the Holy Ghost, that testimony burns into the person's heart and is not easily destroyed. (*Theodore M. Burton*, GGG, p. 61.)

(7A-6) *It does not come from preparation in earthly things.* The power to bear testimony, the ability and the feeling of being able to say that one knows that Jesus is the Christ and that the restoration of the gospel has come through the hands of Joseph Smith, comes entirely by the power of the Holy Ghost. That power does not come through any education or through any special preparation on the part of the recipient in earthly things, but rather it whispers into the heart of the one who wants to know, and once whispered and once understood, that person may stand and say as surely as I or anyone else may stand and say it, that he knows that Jesus is the Christ. (*S. Dilworth Young*, CR, Oct. 1955, pp. 103-104.)

(7A-7) *Unless the Spirit of God carries the message the truth will never be understood.* The things of God can only be known by the Spirit or through the Spirit of God. It doesn't matter how good, ethical, moral, decent, or brilliant the individual is, unless the Spirit of God carries the message the truth will never be understood. That message is all through these books. Paul was writing about it two thousand years ago, trying to help the Corinthians understand that just being very bright in the head was not enough. Just being extremely well educated is not enough. Just being good and decent and even noble and lofty in life and concept — these are not enough. What we have to have to understand the things of the Spirit is the Spirit. That is what Paul meant in the first book to the Corinthians in the second chapter when, after talking about things greater than eye hath seen or ear heard or that have ever entered into the heart of man, he said that we know them through the Spirit. . . . He explained that the natural man — that means the man without God, without the Spirit in this world, according to great prophets — just can't understand these things. "Neither can ye know them, because they are spiritually discerned." In that little line is a very great lot of sense. I plead with you to know it. It may save your life, because if you are alert and awake you will find questions of magnitude that can only be answered through that Spirit. (*Marion D. Hanks,* UU, 12 May 1978, pp. 3-5.)

(7A-8) *Many of us have the same problem that Nicodemus had.* Of course we must study. We must put forth effort. But we shall not acquire a knowledge of the truth only through the reasoning of our minds, although that may lead us to an appreciation for the Church. But the knowledge, the sure and certain knowledge, comes as a gift from the Lord. . . .

The Lord taught this great lesson in his conversation with Nicodemus, a ruler of the Jews who came to him by night. Jesus explained that he must be born again of the water and of the spirit, and then went on to say, "That which is born of the flesh is flesh; and that which is born of the spirit is spirit. Marvel not that I said unto thee, Ye must be born again."

And then note these interesting words. The Lord said, "The wind bloweth where it listeth, and thou hearest the sound thereof, but canst not tell whence it cometh, and whither it goeth; so is every one that is born of the Spirit." (John 3:8.)

Many of us have the same problem that Nicodemus had. As the Savior explained, we hear the sound of the wind and cannot tell whence it cometh or whither it goeth, but we are unwilling to accept this. We want to discover by finite reasoning that which comes as a gift from the Infinite. (*Gordon B. Hinckley,* ACR, Aug. 1975 — Seoul, Korea, p. 12.)

(7A-9) *God cannot be found through research alone.* It should be kept in mind that God cannot be found through research alone, nor his gospel understood and appreciated by study only, for no one may know the Father or the Son but "he to whom the Son will reveal him." (Luke 10:22.) The skeptic will some day either in time or eternity learn to his sorrow that his egotism has robbed him of much joy and growth, and that as has been decreed by the Lord: The things of God cannot be understood by the spirit of man; that man cannot by himself find out God or his program; that no amount of research nor rationalizing will bring a testimony, but it must come through the heart when compliance with the program has made the person eligible to receive that reward. The Savior could have taken highly trained minds from the temple porches for the chief builders of his kingdom, but he went to the seashore to get humble fishermen. He wanted men who would not depend upon their own intellects *only* to ferret out the truths, but unbiased men to whom he might reveal his new program, men who were trusting and sincere and willing to serve. (*Spencer W. Kimball*, CR, Oct. 1944, pp. 44-45.)

(7A-10) *Then he knows what the world does not know.* When a man receives the surety in his heart that this work is true, when he gains a testimony by the power of the Holy Ghost, then he knows what the world does not know, and he can go forth and bear record of it to them.

We are not concerned particularly or especially with the matter of intellectuality. Everything pertaining to the gospel is rational and reasonable. It is intellectual in the sense that we can sustain it by sense and reason and wisdom, but religion is something far more than intellectuality. Religion is a matter of revelation, of spirituality. Religion comes from God, and those who receive it become living witnesses of its truth and divinity. (*Bruce R. McConkie*, CR, Oct. 1969, p. 83.)

(7A-11) *Blazing a trail, and marking out the way.* Mormonism has in its hand the mightiest weapons that man can wield, divine authority and the power of pure testimony that cuts like a keen two-edged sword. Argument has its mission, and God can inspire an argument just as readily as He can a testimony; but there is something peculiar about the power of testimony. It is a pioneer. Argument may come afterwards and fill up the gaps, build the bridges and the cities; but testimony goes before into the wilderness blazing a trail, and marking out the way. (*Orson F. Whitney*, CR, Apr. 1912, p. 47.)

(7A-12) *An unlettered person enlightened direct from God will know more.*
No man by his own researches can find out God. He may, by reason and
reflection, by observing and pondering upon the wonders of creation, by
studying his own internal and external nature, come to the sure conclusion that there is a God, and to a very small extent make an estimate of
his character. But without the Almighty manifests himself in some
manner, finite man can never obtain a knowledge of infinite Deity.
The speculations of human beings concerning God are many and
various, and a vast number of their conclusions inconsistent and vain.
Human learning, no matter how extensive, and human research, no
matter how profound, are of necessity inadequate alone to the acquisition of a knowledge of divine things. Hence an unlettered person
enlightened direct from God, will know more of Deity than the most
erudite collegian who has not received this divine illumination.
(*Charles W. Penrose, MD, p. 11.*)

(7A-13) *A rash and ill-considered statement.* We are asked by one of our
brethren whether it is possible for a man, by means of his five senses
alone, independent of the Holy Ghost, to know that Joseph Smith is a
prophet of the Living God, as he says one of the brethren has asserted
that he had this testimony through his outer senses. . . . Paul says: "No
man can say that Jesus is the Lord, but by the Holy Ghost." The same
may be said in relation to the knowledge of Joseph Smith being a
prophet of God.

For a man to say he knows a spiritual truth by the aid of his outer
senses is a rash and ill-considered expression, and it should not give rise
to discussion, but should be understood as being made without due
consideration. (*George Q. Cannon, JI, 15 Oct. 1890, p. 627.*)

(7A-14) *Spiritual light versus natural light.* As the light of the sun reveals
natural objects to our eyes, so the spirit that comes from God, with a
fitting place to occupy and conditions to operate in, reveals the things
of God. We see natural things by the light of the sun. We see spiritual
things by spiritual light, and he that is spiritual discerneth all things and
judgeth all things, and he that is not spiritual cannot comprehend
spiritual things. They are foolishness to him. (*Charles W. Penrose, DW,
10 Dec. 1884, p. 738.*)

(7A-15) *We must know our own spiritual senses.* Our physical senses,
such as seeing, hearing, feeling, tasting, and smelling, form the foun-

dation for our testifying to physical facts. To be a competent witness, however, of spiritual knowledge, we can rely upon all of these physical means so far as we are capable, but in addition to all that, we must have an added qualification. We must have a spiritual sense which we feel, and which is as real to us as any of these physical senses of which I have spoken. These spiritual senses, which we must realize through the sense of feeling, we must know in our mortal existence. (*Henry D. Moyle*, MI, p. 108.)

B. Relative Value of Various Types of Knowledge

(7B-1) *We must keep spiritual and intellectual in balance.* I listened some years ago to a startling confession of a man who stood in a high place. I shall speak carefully of this, lest you try to identify him. He said he had gone to a midwest university, where he received his Ph.D. in education. His father, who was in the Presidency of the Church, went to his graduation exercises and, after the exercises were over, took him to lunch and said to him, "My boy, for eight years now you have done very little in the Church. You have gone through your college years, and now you have gone through your Ph.D. years, and you haven't been very active in the Church. I want you to promise me that when you get back home you will get active in the Church."

But the son said, "When I returned home, to my shocking surprise, the boys with whom I had graduated from high school had grown spiritually until they were Ph.D.'s in religion, but I was still in the high school age. I had laid aside my religion for eight years."

As I listened to that rather sad confession, and being closely associated with that man, I watched him go through the rest of his life. He never did have his spiritual self catch up with that intellectual side. The result was that he failed to take the counsel of his father. He went through life making decisions by his own measure of what was right and wrong, and finally he lost his place in the Church and was excommunicated because of his conduct. I say, as you think of that, it should be a warning to all of us that we must keep our spiritual selves as alive and growing as our intellectual selves. (*Harold B. Lee*, BYU, 1973, pp. 89-90.)

(7B-2) *The importance of spiritual knowledge.* Desirable as is secular knowledge, one is not truly educated unless he has the spiritual with the secular. The secular knowledge is to be desired; the spiritual knowledge is an absolute necessity. We shall need all of the accumulated secular knowledge in order to create worlds and to furnish them, but only through the "mysteries of God" and these hidden treasures of knowledge may we arrive at the place and condition where we may use that knowledge in creation and exaltation. (*Spencer W. Kimball,* CR, Oct. 1968, p. 131.)

(7B-3) *An expert in the spiritual field.* The expert in the scientific field is one who by his experimentation has come to know that an announced theory is true. An "expert," so-called, in the spiritual world is in the making when he, by humility and faith, knows that God hears and answers prayer. Such a one has "arrived" when he has an unshakable testimony that God is our Father and that through His Son, Jesus Christ, all mankind may be saved by obedience to the laws and ordinances of the gospel. The Lord has given the inspired truth that "it is impossible for a man to be saved in ignorance." (Doctrine and Covenants 131:6.) Does this mean that one must be a college graduate or a man of letters to be saved? Not at all. Man cannot be saved in ignorance of those saving principles of the gospel of Jesus Christ even if he were to have all the book learning in the world. We have been plainly taught by the leaders of this dispensation that "the principle of knowledge is the principle of salvation . . . [and that] the principle of salvation is given us through the knowledge of Jesus Christ." (*Joseph Smith's Teachings,* p. 297.) "Reading the experiences of others, or the revelation given to *them* can never give *us* a comprehensive view of our condition and true relation to God. Knowledge of these things can only be obtained by experience through ordinances of God set forth for that purpose." (p. 324.) But the Lord has encouraged us to strive diligently for knowledge and intelligence from every source. Here are the Prophet's inspired words of counsel: "Whatever principle of intelligence we attain unto in this life, it will rise with us in the resurrection. And if a person gains more knowledge and intelligence in this life through his diligence and obedience than another, he will have so much the advantage in the world to come." (Doctrine and Covenants 130:18-19.) (*Harold B. Lee,* SHP, pp. 76-77.)

C. The Necessity of Spiritual Experiences

(7C-1) *Identifying spiritually endowed people.* Well, a testimony is the beginning of revelation. It is where we start. Let me illustrate what is involved. The Lord would not have done this, but for illustration purposes let us say he might. The Lord might have said, "I am going to save people on earth who have physical ability." Then he would say to the Elders of Israel, "Go out and find the people who have physical ability and when you have found them, bring them into this organization and I will save them in the Celestial Kingdom." Now if he had done that, what would we have had to do to find people with physical ability? I do not think we would have gone out and talked about physical things. Anybody can talk about physical things. If we wanted to find the athletes, we would get them involved in a contest. They would have to have a physical experience and demonstrate that they had physical capacity, and then we would identify them and we would bring them into the Church. That is one illustration. There is another one.

The Lord might have said, but he did not, "I am going to save the people on earth who have intellectual capacity. Salvation will be based on intellectual things: knowledge, reason, sense, judgment." And then he would have said, "Go out and pick out the people who have intellectual capacity and bring them into this organization and I will save them." Now, how do you find somebody who has intellectual ability? It is not by talking about things; it is by taking an examination, by undergoing an experience, by testing so that you identify who is intellectual and what capacities they have.

Suppose the Lord had said, "I am going to save everybody on earth who has musical talent, or who develops it," and then had told us, as his representatives, "Go out and find the people who have musical talent." How would we do it? Not by talking about music, but by getting people involved in a musical experience. We would audition them; we would put them in a choir; we would get them to demonstrate what their voices were like.

Well, what the Lord actually said was, "I am going to save the people who have spiritual power, who have spiritual capacity." He said, "My sheep hear my voice." (John 10:27.) "Now you Elders of Israel, go out among the hosts of men and find the people who are spiritually endowed." How do you do it? If you are sectarian, what you do is you get involved in intellectual things and you talk about religion, and anybody can talk *about* religion.

I happen to be tone deaf, or virtually so, but I can talk about music. Such is no problem at all. I can talk for hours about music. That is not the issue; it does not make me a musician. And similarly it is not talking *about* religion that identifies spiritual people. The only way that you identify spiritually endowed people is to get them involved in a spiritual experience. Something has to happen in their lives. They have to be fed spiritually. You are fed spiritually when you hear testimonies, when you pray, when you worship, when you do a great variety of things that the Church provides, things that enable you to get in tune with the mind and will of the Lord. We bear testimony, and we counsel the people to do this and this and this, to have the Spirit of the Lord as a companion.

You must get a spiritual experience; you must get revelation. Nobody really gets a spiritual experience of any magnitude until he gets a revelation from the Holy Spirit. And, if you have had a revelation, then you have had a spiritual experience. If you have not had a revelation, you need to follow the formula and the pattern that the Lord has provided so that you get a spiritual experience. Once you get a spiritual experience and follow the pattern and you know what to do, then you apply those same rules and regulations and pursue that same course, and you can get revelation on added things. That, of course, is what Joseph Smith did. He grew in the things of the Spirit. At first he used the Urim and Thummim; later he did not have to use it. He first got revelation with great effort and great labor and, pretty soon, he had the spiritual stature when things came much easier to him. We can grow in this knowledge. (*Bruce R. McConkie*, UU, 22 Jan. 1971, pp. 5-6.)

(7C-2) *You haven't been in the Church yet.* I had an experience some years ago with a person who was acquainted with someone who went to this institution. The young man was brought up in the Church and he came here and began to get his education and his bent was philosophy, and it wasn't too long before he didn't know what was true and what wasn't true. He reached the point where he doubted himself. He wasn't sure whether he had a testimony or whether the Church was true. A friend of mine who had received a doctorate in philosophy from an eastern institution was called in to see if he could help this young man. They sat

down and chatted together and then my friend asked this young man a
series of about ten or twelve questions to see if he had had any spiritual
experiences in his life. And this particular person had to answer "no" in
every case, except for "maybe" in one or two cases. Have you ever had
an answer to your prayers, or have you seen someone healed by the
power of the priesthood — things like that. And he could not answer
yes. My friend looked at this young man and said, "How can you leave
the Church when you haven't been in it yet?" And I think that was a
very telling comment. The power, the vitality, the truth of the gospel of
Jesus Christ lies with the spiritual experiences and the spiritual blessings
found within the Church. More specifically it lies with a testimony
which is the greatest spiritual blessing of all. This testimony *must* reside
in the heart of each member. (*Loren C. Dunn*, UU, 1 Feb. 1974, p. 1.)

(7C-3) *What counts is to become a personal participant.* We need *religious
experience*, we need to become personally involved with God — our
concern is not to read what somebody has said *about* religion. I read
frequently, but primarily for amusement or diversion, what somebody
has said in a critical vein about the Church or what some Protestant
professor of religion has said about the tenets of Christianity. Actually
what they say — their views are not worth the snap of the fingers as far as
importance is concerned. It is totally immaterial what somebody has to
say about the Church in a critical vein, who is writing to evaluate from
an intellectual standpoint a doctrine or a practice or a so-called program
of the Church — it is just totally inconsequential as far as the Church is
concerned and as its spiritually inclined people are concerned. Religion
is not a matter of the intellect.

I repeat, that the better the intellect, the more we are able to evaluate
spiritual principles, and it is a marvelous thing to be learned and
educated and have insight and mental capacity, because we can use
these talents and abilities in the spiritual realm. *But what counts in the
field of religion is to become a personal participant in it.* Instead of reading all
that has been written and evaluating all that all the scholars of all the
world have said about heaven and hell, we need to do what the Prophet
said: gaze five minutes into heaven. As a consequence, we would know
more than all that has ever been evaluated and written and analyzed on
the subject.

Religion is a matter of getting the Holy Ghost into the life of an individual.

We study, of course, and we need to evaluate. And by virtue of our study we come up with some foundations that get us into the frame of mind so that we *can* seek the things of the Spirit. But in the end the result is *getting our souls touched by the Spirit of God.* (*Bruce R. McConkie,* BYU, 11 Oct. 1966, pp. 7-8.)

(7C-4) *"Two churches" within the Church.* I believe there are two churches in our Church. On the one side I see an organization that I will refer to as the Mormon Church. This is the outward organization. These are the programs of the Church. This is the structure of the Church that can be seen by the world. I might add that I don't use the word "Mormon" too endearingly, mainly because the Lord has told us through the Book of Mormon that his Church will bear his name, but if it has the name of a man, then it will be the church of the man. (3 Nephi 27:8.) Now Mormon was a great prophet, but, nonetheless, he was a man. This is not the Mormon Church. This is the Church of Jesus Christ.

Still I see the outward organization on the one side and I will refer to it as the Mormon Church. On the other side, I see what I like to refer to as the Church of Jesus Christ. Here are the spiritual blessings of the Church; here is the power and influence of revelation. Here is the power of the priesthood; here is the strength and vitality of the Church. It cannot be seen by the world; it has to be experienced in order for a person to know that it is there.

So you have the two organizations: on the one hand, the Mormon Church, as I would call it; on the other hand, the Church of Jesus Christ. The Mormon Church is the organization that the world sees. Some of those who are impressed by how we function, feel that they can come to us and say, "How do you do it?" and we can give them a simple formula and they can go back and apply it in their own organization. But it doesn't work that way, does it? The true vitality and strength of the Church is found in what I call the Church of Jesus Christ.

The problem that we face sometimes is that there are some members of the Church who feel they are members of what I refer to as the Mormon Church or this outward organization. These are the people that I suspect have not experienced or have not recognized the spiritual blessings of the Church. These are the people who feel that if they write enough letters to the President of the Church, a doctrine can be changed because that is the way the world does it. These are the people that possibly don't see to the heart of the Church, and haven't taken opportunity to receive the blessings that are existent for all people who will come and accept the gospel of Jesus Christ.

So I believe it is important for us to know where we stand between these two organizations within our own Church, whether we are closer to the outward organization, whether the Church is more of a social matter to us, or whether we have partaken of and enjoyed the spiritual blessings of the gospel of Jesus Christ. It is good for us to know, in our lives, where we stand between these two points. (*Loren C. Dunn*, BYU, 24 Mar. 1970, pp. 2-3.)

D.   Testimonies and Scientific Proof

(7D-1) *Is a testimony susceptible to proof?* Is this that we call testimony susceptible of definite, tangible proof? To me it is. I recognize that by the use of my ordinary senses — hearing, smelling, seeing, and touch, I demonstrate the existence of things. I prove to my satisfaction their materiality and the operation of the laws of nature so far as I know them. To me the operations of the Spirit of God within the structure of my life are as tangible, as susceptible of definite, concrete proof as the operations of many of the laws of nature. When I respond to this that I call my testimony, my heart warms, my body thrills. I feel the tingle of it. A satisfaction, a peace, a contentment, a joy that transcends description, envelops me. It is the proof to me that it is there, and so I assert it is susceptible of tangible proof and demonstration. Is it susceptible of scientific analysis? Yes, if the scientist will apply the test which is prescribed to demonstrate its truth. We may say to any scientist, to any man who inquires, just what God has said: "If you do my work and my will and keep my commandments you shall know whether it be the work of God or man." Are we justified in taking any other method than the method prescribed to determine the existence of testimony? I leave that thought for the reflection of those who would test the actuality of a testimony, for I know it will come to every one who applies the prescribed method of attaining it. (*Stephen L Richards*, CR, Oct. 1925, p. 119.)

(7D-2) *Placing unwarranted limitations on another's power.* Because one does not receive this positive assurance is no reason why another cannot. To say that another person cannot see the light because you fail to comprehend it is to place unwarranted limitations on another's power. To say that no one can know of the doctrine because you do not is like saying that there is no germ or virus because it is not visible to you, and is to deny the word of God. (*Spencer W. Kimball,* CR, Oct. 1944, p. 45.)

(7D-3) *The testimony of a single witness with the facts.* I have interviewed hundreds of . . . [returned missionaries] . . . and on questioning, at least ninety-nine percent of them readily and positively declared they knew certainly that God lives and that the Church of Jesus Christ of Latter-day Saints is his Church. Were these young people telling the truth? Did they, and can any one, positively know that God lives? Multitudes of worldly people answer, nay. But in such a case a negative answer has no value. All it can do is to show that the witness is without knowledge. The testimony of a single witness who has the facts far outweighs the testimony of the multitudes who have no facts. (*Joseph F. Merrill,* CR, Oct. 1948, p. 58.)

(7D-4) *If I bear such a witness, it stands against them.* I can stand in the congregations of the earth and can reason with the people out of the revelations. I can cite the scriptures of old. I can recite the proofs and the evidences, the fruits such as the Book of Mormon, which have flown from the ministry of Joseph Smith. When I do this, if people are not spiritually inclined, they can argue and contend and attempt to explain these things away. But, having done all this, having set the stage, having laid a foundation, if I then say to the people: "In addition to all these evidences, I have received revelation that has come to me by the power of the Holy Ghost, telling me that this latter-day work is true, and I bear record to you that God has spoken in this day; now, if you will heed my warning voice and come and investigate and learn for yourselves, you also can know the divinity of the work" — if I bear such a witness, that witness stands against them at the judgment bar of the Almighty. (*Bruce R. McConkie,* CR, Oct. 1962, p. 10.)

(7D-5) *Their method is without honor.* There are those who presume to judge the gospel and the testimonies of Church members upon purely theoretical grounds. They do not have a strong desire for truth, will not pray, nor will they give ample study to the system. Least of all will they practice the precepts of the gospel. Such judges deserve perhaps more pity than ridicule. Their method is without honor in the halls of truth. (*John A. Widtsoe*, IE, May 1943, p. 289.)

(7D-6) *One of the wonders and the glories and the beauties of a testimony.* You can't argue with a testimony. That is one of the wonders and the glories and the beauties of a testimony. If I quote a scripture to you and say to you that it means thus and thus, and someone comes along and says, "That's all very interesting, but I think it means this and that," you have a religious contention on your hands. But if, instead of that alone, if I first quote the scripture and then say, "Now I know by the revelations of the Holy Spirit to my soul that such and such is true," you can't debate that. If I say, "I know by the power of the Holy Spirit that the Father and the Son appeared to Joseph Smith," there is nothing to argue about. It has become a personal, subjective thing. You can say, "Well, he's mad; he's insane, he's deluded." You can say, "He's wrong," but there is nothing else to debate. You don't debate a testimony. (*Bruce R. McConkie*, ACR, Feb. 1976 — Sydney, Australia, pp. 18-19.)

(7D-7) *Scientific knowledge versus spiritual knowledge.* I gratefully acknowledge the contributions which science and scholarly men have made to an understanding of the universe and its physical and astronomical laws and phenomena. What a boon to humanity these contributions have been! But, with all his long quest, and the knowledge and control of the great forces of the universe he has attained, does man yet understand the real inner essence of these hidden forces? What about gravitation, heat, light, and electricity — these physical forces which we all know and around each of which an elaborate science has developed? Intelligent man has discovered how to measure them, many of their properties and attributes and how to utilize them, but has he yet found out just what the basic primal element in each of these forces is? I think the greatest of the scientists have sufficient humility and frankness to admit that the ultimate has not yet been achieved and that these basic facts are still beyond them and the search goes on and on.

Now, if we admit our inability to fully comprehend and define these material forces about us which we know so tangibly and definitely by the effects which they produce, why, I ask you, should we be so reluctant to acknowledge the existence and potency of other hidden forces which affect the lives and conduct of men and women but which, like these other manifestations of nature, we cannot fully understand and define with human faculties? It seems to me this is a legitimate question to ask a man of reason and logic. If he should reply, "I have no knowledge of spiritual forces because I've had no experience with them — therefore, for me, they do not exist," I should have no quarrel with him. That may well be his status. But if he should say that such spiritual forces have no reality for *others* and that they are mere imaginary concoctions of the mind, then I should brand him as unscientific and illogical — first, because he presumes to say that a thing may not be because he doesn't understand it; and secondly, because without experience himself, he denies the validity of the experiences of others. I think that, fortunately, there are not a great many who take such a pronounced position, but I regret to note that there are many who exhibit such an indifferent and disparaging attitude toward spiritual concepts and those who hold them as to mark them with an intolerance and presumption they would not relish in others.

So, my friends, I submit the conclusion that a testimony of spiritual things is not unreasonable and that it is a great mistake to impugn the intelligence of anyone who has such conviction. We take the position in our Church that there is no higher order of intelligence than that which comprehends and accepts spiritual truth and that in its final analysis all truth is spiritual. Our scriptures declare that all things were created spiritually before they were created temporally, and that "truth is knowledge of things as they are and as they were and as they are to come, . . . the spirit of truth is of God." (*Stephen L Richards*, CN, 16 Jan. 1943, p. 7.)

8

MAINTAINING A STRONG TESTIMONY

A. A Testimony Is Continually Changing

(8A-1) *It is much like a living thing.* Since a testimony is a compound of knowledge and the use of knowledge, it is much as a living thing. It is never static, like a stone. The small testimony may grow larger, the large testimony smaller. Therefore, it must be cared for, as any other type of life. Our treatment of it is of prime importance. (*John A. Widtsoe, IE, May 1945, p. 273.*)

(8A-2) *It is as hard to hold as a moonbeam.* Testimony isn't something you have today, and you are going to have always. A testimony is fragile. It is as hard to hold as a moonbeam. It is something you have to recapture every day of your life.

We keep our testimonies by living, praying and being active in the Church and by keeping the commandments of God. It is then that the guiding spirit will be with us, one of the most prized possessions a member of the Church can have. (*Harold B. Lee, CN, 15 July 1972, p. 4.*)

(8A-3) *A testimony is never static.* Some members of the Church possess powerful and unfaltering testimonies, while others possess less forceful testimonies. It should be recognized that testimonies can be acquired, testimonies can be kept, and testimonies can be lost. . . .

To those of you who feel that you have a firm testimony, remember: a testimony is never static; a testimony can be lost. To keep it alive, it must be fed. Continue to study, pray, attend church, and be involved. This will not only keep your testimony alive, but it will expand and become more meaningful in your life. (*Franklin D. Richards*, CR, Apr. 1974, pp. 84, 86.)

(8A-4) *Testimony of today will not be the testimony of tomorrow.* One day while the Master and his disciples were on their way to Caesarea Philippi, they stopped for a rest. And the Master asked them, "Whom do men say that I the Son of man am? And they said, Some say that thou art John the Baptist: some, Elias; and others, Jeremias, or one of the prophets."

And then Jesus asked the disciples to bear their testimonies: "But whom say ye that I am?"

I suppose they all bore testimony, but we have only Peter's recorded. "Thou art the Christ, the Son of the living God."

Then the Master replied, "Blessed art thou, Simon Barjona: for flesh and blood hath not revealed it unto thee, but my Father which is in heaven." (Matthew 16:13-17.)

Peter had received a revelation. He knew that Jesus was the Christ, the Savior of the world, the divine Son of God. Now, it could only have been a year or so after this incident when the Master turned to Peter with a rebuke. We do not know what it was that caused him to rebuke Simon Peter, but he said: "Simon, Simon, behold, Satan hath desired to have you, that he may sift you as wheat: But I have prayed for thee, that thy faith fail not: and *when thou art converted, strengthen thy brethren.*" (Luke 22:31-32. Italics added.)

Can you imagine the Lord saying this to his chief apostle, to the very man who had previously received a revelation as to the divine mission of the Lord? The Lord said to Peter that Satan just about had him, and that he had better go out and get converted. Well we might ask, "What does it mean to become converted?" especially after we learn the Lord had suggested that Peter was becoming unconverted. In effect, the Lord is saying that the testimony you have today will not be your testimony of tomorrow. Your testimony is either going to grow and grow until it becomes as the brightness of the sun, or it is going to diminish to nothing, depending on what you do about it. Peter, somehow, was losing his testimony. (*Harold B. Lee*, NE, Feb. 1971, pp. 2-3.)

(8A-5) *If we are not growing, we are dying.* Sometimes men say, "I have a testimony of the Gospel." I believe them. Sometimes I hear them say, "I know the Gospel is true," and I believe them. But . . . I have said time and again . . . , "When I hear you say 'I know the Gospel is true,' I would like to stop you and have you repeat that but say only, 'I know the Gospel.' " Of course it is true if it is the Gospel, but do you know the Gospel?

And that brings us to the point of how much are we converted after all? And, to what are we converted? Now if we are not growing, I repeat, we are dying, and a testimony can be taken away from a man. (*Hugh B. Brown*, UA-CHD, 18 Mar. 1961 — Leicester, England, pp. 7-8.)

B.   Testimonies Require Nourishment

(8B-1) *A testimony must be fed, cared for and nurtured.* A testimony is a living thing, not a static, dead thing — it is alive and sometimes fills a man and a woman until the visions of heaven are opened to him or her. By that token of life, a testimony must be fed, cared for and nurtured, kept in its right place and position, protected if needs be. (*John A. Widtsoe*, CR, Apr. 1951, p. 101.)

(8B-2) *A testimony needs to be constantly reinforced.* A personal testimony after we have received it, I have learned, and I am grateful that I have learned it, needs to be constantly reinforced. . . . It may have been acquired through study and prayer, but if our testimony ceases to grow, it may finally cease to be.

Therefore, it requires each of us daily to try to improve our lives, strive to discipline ourselves and properly to conduct our behavior.

Our testimony needs to be constantly cultivated and strengthened to remain forceful and alive. (*Thorpe B. Isaacson*, CR, Oct. 1952, p. 64.)

(8B-3) *Do not neglect to nourish that tree by searching the scriptures regularly.* Those who have planted the seed of the gospel and have worked to grow a tree of testimony often neglect to nourish that tree. We do this at our peril, for "when the heat of the sun cometh and scorcheth it," we may "pluck it up and cast it out," thinking the tree has no value. (See Alma 32:38.) Each of us will have our own experiences that will constitute the coming of "the heat of the sun," and these experiences will most likely come to us when we least want them or are least prepared!

The gospel has a rolling relevancy to life if we search the scriptures regularly. Unstudied and unapplied dormant doctrines will seem to wither and shrink in importance and relevance, and this is the atrophy that precedes indifference or apostasy. Keeping the tree of testimony alive, according to Alma, requires "faith . . . diligence . . . patience, and long suffering." (See Alma 32:43.) (*Neal A. Maxwell*, IN, Nov. 1970, p. 405.)

(8B-4) *A testimony will grow dim if not nourished.* The strength of a personal testimony to the individual is of surpassing value and will abide with all who keep the commandments of the Lord. But that testimony will grow dim if not nourished by the proper conduct of life and activity in our Heavenly Father's work. (*Harold B. Lee*, EN, Feb. 1974, p. 77.)

(8B-5) *There is no guarantee that this testimony will remain steadfast.* A testimony is a priceless gift from God. But even though a person may receive a witness through the Holy Ghost, there is no guarantee that this testimony will remain steadfast unless the person exerts constant effort to keep that testimony alive. Testimonies gained may be lost through carelessness, indifference, and/or neglect.

Testimonies need to be nourished and fed. President Lee wisely counseled: "If we are not reading the scriptures daily, our testimonies are growing thinner, our spirituality isn't increasing in depth." (Seminar for Regional Representatives of the Twelve, December 12, 1970.) (*Henry D. Taylor*, CR, Apr. 1971, p. 160.)

(8B-6) *If neglected, it will not remain.* The man who professes a testimony . . . and who assumes that his testimony embraces all knowledge he needs, and who therefore lives in indolence and ignorance, shall surely discover his error to his own cost and loss. A gift from God, if neglected, or unworthily used, is in time withdrawn; the testimony of the truth will not remain with one who, having received, uses not the sacred gift in the cause of individual and general advancement. (*Joseph F. Smith*, JI, 1 Aug. 1906, p. 465.)

(8B-7) *When there beat in your hearts a witness and a testimony.* But as I see those who are here today, I think of many who were once faithful and active who have now dropped away. In the hope that some few of these may be present with us, I make a plea to them. Come back. You were never happier in all your lives than you were when you were walking in the fellowship of the Saints, when you were observing the teachings of the gospel, and when there beat in your hearts a witness and testimony of the truth of this great latter-day work. Here is where your happiness is to be found. Here is where you will find peace and growth and love. And you will come to know again the sweet companionship of the Holy Spirit. Your brethren and sisters extend their hands in warm welcome. Come back.

A man may receive a testimony of this work, but he can keep it only if he feeds it. He must nurture it and exercise it. (*Gordon B. Hinckley*, ACR, Aug. 1975 — Hong Kong, p. 3.)

C. Ways of Strengthening a Testimony

(8C-1) *Like a muscle it grows stronger with use.* Don't you think that you can go three, and six, and nine months and twelve months without bearing your testimony and still keep its full value. It is like my voice. You probably notice how weak it is when I start, but it gets stronger as I go. And it is like your muscle — your testimony is the same — you use it, and it becomes strong. You use your testimony, and it grows. You fail to use it, and it goes out of being entirely. (*Spencer W. Kimball*, UA-CHD, 2 Jan. 1959 — Los Angeles, Calif., p. 16.)

(8C-2) *God's ways are not man's ways.* If you would keep your testimony, give it away; give it away. God's ways are not man's ways. The mind of man would say, "If you want to keep something, put it in the bank and hoard it; lock it up with a key." But the Lord says, "If you want to keep these spiritual gifts, you don't hoard them and lock them up. You give them away and share them with other people." (*Robert L. Simpson*, UA-CHD, 22 Aug. 1973 — Provo, Utah, p. 12.)

(8C-3) *How may a testimony be kept?* First, to keep our testimony we must feed it, regularly and plentifully. The steps that lead to a testimony: desire, prayer, study, and practice, must be trodden continuously. The desire for truth should stamp our every act; help from God in all things must be invoked; the study of the gospel, which has not been plumbed to its depth by any man, should be continued; and the practice of gospel principles, in all our labors, must never be forgotten.

He who would retain his testimony is required to give constant study to the gospel. He cannot live forever on that which he learned yesterday. By a little such study every day, light will follow light, and understanding will increase. This is doubly important since we live in a changing world, which requires continuous applications of gospel truth to new conditions.

To keep his testimony, a person must increase in the use of gospel principles. There must be stricter conformity with the higher as well as the lesser laws of life — more activity in Church service; increasing charity and kindness; greater sacrifice for the common good; more readiness to help advance the plan of salvation; more truth in all we do. And, as our knowledge of gospel law increases, our activity under gospel law must increase.

By such feeding, a testimony may be kept; may remain whole and sound; and may grow to become an increasingly certain guide, and a constant joy in life. There is no other way to preserve a testimony. (*John A. Widtsoe*, IE, May 1945, p. 273.)

(8C-4) *Things to do to strengthen a testimony.* To any of you — either here or at home — who do not have a testimony or who would like to strengthen your testimony, I would recommend a few things that you can do to develop or strengthen a testimony.

1. Study the scriptures and other books written by Church leaders.
2. Keep the commandments, which include loving thy neighbor as thyself, being honest and upright, paying a full tithing, and keeping morally clean.
3. Attend sacrament meeting and other Church meetings, in which you can listen to the testimonies of the faithful members of the Church.
4. Associate with good people.
5. Stay out of the devil's territory by shunning evil.
6. Repent of all sins and imperfections, and repentance includes both confession and forsaking of such sins.
7. Pray to the Lord. . . .

Once we have developed and obtained a testimony, we can never cease working to strengthen it. . . . We must continue to study, to pray, to obey the commandments, so that the Holy Ghost will continue to strengthen our testimony. When a testimony is not growing, it is in danger of becoming weaker. (O. *Leslie Stone*, CR, Apr. 1975, pp. 10-11.)

(8C-5) *He will receive continual additions.* When a person receives intelligence from the Lord, and is willing to communicate that for the benefit of the people, he will receive continual additions to that intelligence; and there is no end to his increase so long as he will hold fast to the faith of the Lord Jesus Christ. (*Lorenzo Snow*, DW, 6 May 1857, p. 67.)

(8C-6) *Your testimony must be shared to survive.* Your testimony must be shared to survive. Any man that harbors his testimony and keeps it hidden and closed in, will one day look and find that his testimony doesn't exist. It's only in giving it away that we maintain it, that it is allowed to flourish and grow, and that it becomes a real part of our heart and soul. (*Robert L. Simpson*, UU, 2 Nov. 1973, pp. 8-9.)

(8C-7) *Formula for growth.* I have discovered, as you have, I am quite sure, the method by which . . . a testimony may be kept alive, blossoming, useful in human life. The formula is simple: Live the gospel every day, practice it, and study it regularly; do not let the affairs of the day that deal with the making of our temporal living crowd aside matters that pertain to the gospel. If we use this formula, our testimony will become increasingly certain, will grow, will expand in meaning and comprehension. (*John A. Widtsoe*, CR, Oct. 1943, p. 112.)

(8C-8) *Expressing our testimonies through service.* As the contrasts between the ways of the world and the ways of God become sharpened by circumstances, the faith of the members of the Church will be tried even more severely. One of the most vital things we can do is to express our testimonies through service, which will, in turn, produce spiritual growth, greater commitment, and a greater capacity to keep the commandments. (*Spencer W. Kimball*, EN, Dec. 1974, p. 5.)

(8C-9) *He who adds not lacks power to maintain.* He that would retain his testimony of the gospel of Jesus Christ must daily pursue that course of life that will foster the continuation of the Spirit as an influence and through service and devotion to the Church, his contact with God is real and earnest. The Parable of the Talents is the expression of this law, for he who adds not to his own knowledge and power lacks the strength to hold that which he has. The responsibility for effort rests with the individual. (*Alvin R. Dyer,* TC, p. 158.)

(8C-10) *To hold it, one must bear it often.* To hold his testimony one must bear it often and live worthy of it. The Lord declared his displeasure in the failure of his people to bear testimony. (*Spencer W. Kimball,* CR, Oct. 1944, p. 45.)

(8C-11) *Vitality of a testimony maintained by participation.* But you must participate in the gospel from the very beginning. You can't be a spectator. You must be a part of it. You must be involved in it, and you must participate. You won't get the blessings of the Church and king-dom of God unless you are participating in the Church.

Let me put it another way. You can't maintain your testimony and you can't maintain your spiritual vitality in The Church of Jesus Christ of Latter-day Saints unless you have a job. I believe that to be true. Now, you can say I'm going to Church and I'm doing all these things, but I just don't have a job. That is like standing there and watching the Church walk away from you. You've got to somehow be involved in the Church and kingdom of God to enjoy its blessings. Put another way, you've got to somehow be involved in helping and strengthening the lives of others. All of the jobs we hold in the Church aim us toward each other so that we can help and strengthen and assist each other. We don't get saved as spectators. We get saved as participants. We don't get saved by what we learn in an institute class. We get saved by applying the principles of what we learn in an institute class. We don't get saved entirely by how we feel. We get saved by making sure our actions and spiritual feelings are in harmony. We have to participate; we have to be involved; we have to *do* the thing that the Lord asks us to do and not just hear it or debate it or discuss it or think about it. Ultimately, we have to *do* it, and if it doesn't become a part of our lives, then it has no power over us as far as helping us to gain salvation.

Now, whatever we are called to do, as far as the kingdom and Church of God is concerned, get in and do it. And if we have a job, do it. We must not excuse ourselves. And if we don't have a job, we should ask for one for the sake of our own spiritual welfare. I know you are busy in school, and I know you are busy in other things, but don't excuse yourself from your participation in the Church. I have seen that happen too many times. I saw it happen back east when I was going to graduate school. They justify themselves and say, "Well now, when I am out of school, I'll do it." And then when they get started they say, "Well, when I really get oriented in this new job, because it requires so many hours of me, I'll do it." And later on they say, "Well, so many people look to me for supervision, when I get this stage of my life over with, I'll do it." And then a little later on they will say, "Well, here I am in the upper years of my life. I've got all my children to support and send to school. Just a few more years and then I will get involved again." And a little later on, "Just a little bit longer and then I will be retired and then I will be able to participate in the Church and do the things I am supposed to do." And what has happened? The opportunities have gone and life has gone. Or perhaps the coming the Son of Man is taking place, and a person finds himself not ready.

It is best to participate now, get into the Church now, and not put it off. Now, you could do too much and if you feel you are, discuss it with your branch president. But everybody can do something, and for the sake of your spiritual welfare, it is good to have a job in the Church. (*Loren C. Dunn*, UU, 10 Nov. 1972, pp. 7-8.)

D.   Evaluating the Strength of Your Testimony

(8D-1) *Examine your weapon before the battle.* I have felt on many occasions, . . . that what we need to do, each one of us, is to begin to examine our own testimonies of the truth. After all, with our testimonies as our chief weapon, we go out to battle evil. We speak of a testimony, yes; we say we have a testimony — but is the testimony of a kind that will enable a man to accept and obey the gospel of the Lord Jesus Christ under any and all conditions? It might be good for us Latter-day Saints to begin to re-examine our own testimonies. A man who goes into battle cleanses his sword, looks after his gun, and he is ready for the battle when it comes. We are in the midst of a great battle today, the battle of the ages, foretold by prophets throughout the long ages of the past. We must begin with a certain understanding of the gospel of the Lord Jesus Christ and a willing, ready acceptance of it. . . . There is no other way. But have we done that? Have we looked into our own hearts, to our testimonies, and added that which is wanting, taken out that which is unworthy? We should be fit for the battle. . . .

Let us look into our testimonies. Are they just words on our tongues, or do they really represent our convictions? If they need mending, mend them; if they need building, build them. (*John A. Widtsoe*, CR, Apr. 1951, pp. 100, 102.)

(8D-2) *Are you receiving sufficient incoming experiences?* Alma, in talking to Church members about the need for spiritual rebirth, inquires, "Have ye experienced this mighty change in your hearts?" In a significant amplification of that query, he continues: ". . . If ye have experienced a change of heart, and if ye have felt to sing the song of redeeming love, I would ask, can ye feel so now?"

Sin, and time not well spent, can erode even bright spiritual experiences unless we are constantly active and growing. Further, since our feelings do ebb and flow, we need to be harvesting the fruits of Gospel living now, without inordinate reliance on past experiences for present joy. Previous satisfaction in Church service — isolated by time or inactivity — is not a sufficient basis for faith to meet today's challenges. Without incoming experiences to reinforce us, our faith is often at the mercy of our moods and circumstances. (*Neal A. Maxwell*, TTC, p. 64.)

(8D-3) *Are you borrowing from bygone inspiration?* Man need have no fear of evil, if his testimony is alive — if he is not borrowing from a bygone inspiration. If the Holy Ghost is bearing witness to him today, this very minute, then, he is in tune with God. *This then is how evil is to be overcome.* (*Alvin R. Dyer*, MT, p. 118.)

(8D-4) *No testimony is too strong.* I will give you an experience that came to me from my colleague, Elder Clifford E. Young, a year or so ago. It seems that before President Heber J. Grant passed away, and many of you know that he was ill for many months, but three or four weeks before he passed away, Brother Young was in his home visiting him. President Grant uttered this prayer: "O God, bless me that I shall not lose my testimony and keep faithful to the end!" Here was the prophet of the Lord at that time, holding the keys of the kingdom, praying that he would not lose his testimony, that he would remain faithful to the end, even though he lay on his sickbed and must have known that he would never be well again. (*John Longden*, CR, Oct. 1958, p. 70.)

(8D-5) *A testimony must be brought up to date to include the living prophet.* I believe and know also, by the revelations of the Holy Ghost to my soul, that Joseph Smith was the instrument in his hands of restoring in this day the fulness of those principles and authorities and graces whereby you and I can go back into our Father's kingdom. I testify and know of Joseph Smith, as the inspired document which announced his martyrdom states: "Joseph Smith, the Prophet and Seer of the Lord, has done more, save Jesus only, for the salvation of men in this world, than any other man that ever lived in it."

... And in addition to that, because a testimony must be brought up to date if it is to have any saving force and value in the lives of men, I testify that I know that the keys of the kingdom have continued with the Saints from the days of Joseph Smith, and that . . . [he] . . . who stands at the head today is the Lord's anointed and the Living Oracle.

It is all well and good to sing praises to the ancient prophets and build sepulchres to their names, but there is no salvation in that fact standing alone. If men in this world in our day want to go back to our Father's kingdom, it is incumbent upon them to come to the Living Oracle and have exercised in their behalf the authority of the priesthood. They must accept and live in harmony with the counsels of those men whom God has chosen today.

". . . He that receiveth my servants receiveth me." (Doctrine and Covenants 84:36.) And on the other hand if we do not receive the servants of the Lord, we do not receive the Lord. (*Bruce R. McConkie,* CR, Apr. 1947, pp. 38-39.)

(8D-6) *Is your nest well feathered?* I worry sometimes about people getting sour. People do get sour. With some people, if their nest is well feathered, the Gospel is true. If their nest is not feathered, the Gospel is not true. Do you ever look into yourself and say: Why is the Gospel true? Is it because you have faith, or is it because everything is all right with you? (*Marvin O. Ashton,* CR, Oct. 1939, p. 61.)

(8D-7) *Are we perfecting our testimonies?* There is something about testimony that all of us should know. It is one thing to bear testimony to the truth and divinity of the work, but we do not perfect our testimonies until we get to the point where we can bear witness that the doctrine we proclaim and the truths we have taught are the mind, will, and voice of the Lord — that they are eternally true. No man can do that, of course, unless he gets into a position where he speaks by the power of the Holy Spirit. (*Bruce R. McConkie*, BYU, 4 Jan. 1972, p. 8.)

(8D-8) *In preparation for the Second Coming, examine your testimony.* There are other things that we need to look into as far as our lives are concerned that are important. Number one is the status of our testimony. We need to have the confirmation to our own hearts of the truthfulness of the gospel of Jesus Christ in order to keep the commandments, in order to have that spiritual harmony that is necessary to be one with the saints, and in order to know what we should do. It is easy to get confused if you do not have a testimony. There are a lot of things that are not of a spiritual nature that can confuse us, can muddy up our lives, and sometimes we don't establish the right kind of relationships or we don't set the right kind of order of things in our lives if our testimony has gone begging. So, in preparation for the coming of the Son of Man, and it doesn't matter if he comes in our lifetime or not, we should look to our testimonies and we should decide whether we stand on the strength of our own relationship with the Lord, or whether we have to lean on someone else. It's all right if you do lean on someone else, but work for the day when you can stand on your own feet and bear your own witness and have that spiritual affirmation in your own heart, because every member of the Church (or any soul, for that matter) has that right. (*Loren C. Dunn*, UU, 10 Nov. 1972, pp. 4-5.)

E. Danger Signs of a Weakening Testimony

(8E-1) *A testimony is gradually lost.* We can lose a testimony by losing activity. [A person doesn't lose a testimony] . . . like you lose a dollar, but your activity slackens and often failing to study and failing to take part result in the loss of that testimony. You have to work at it to keep it strong, just like exercise makes a muscle strong. (*Hugh B. Brown*, CN, 26 Oct. 1974, p. 4.)

(8E-2) *There is some "softening up" first.* Often I have asked myself why it is that some people apostatize from the truth. I have never believed that a person falls away suddenly, all at once, any more than a person who has been righteous and honest all his life would go out and suddenly rob a bank. There is some preparatory work in advance. There is some "softening-up" process which leads to the apostate condition. Big sins generally are preceded by little ones, and I believe that this is true with respect to people who fall away from the truth.

Seeds are sown, seeds of doubt, disbelief, distrust, disrespect. These seeds are watered; they are nurtured; and finally they become fully developed until they produce their evil fruit. (*Mark E. Petersen*, CR, Apr. 1953, p. 82.)

(8E-3) *How may a testimony be lost?* A testimony, being a living thing, may die. . . . Refuse to do the things that lead to a testimony, and, gradually, it will starve, wither, and perish. It does not matter how strong it may have been. It must be fed to be kept alive.

Starvation of a testimony usually begins with failure to keep properly in touch with divine forces, to pray. Then, desire to learn and to live the gospel law soon weakens. Sacred covenants are forgotten. Study of the gospel is set aside for some other study or activity. There is less and less participation in the life of the Church. Eyes are blurred so that the laws of life are forgotten.

There are many attacks by the evil one upon a weakening testimony. Commonly, a feeling of superiority, ending in ambition for office, overshadows all else and leads to testimony starvation. Personal ambition has always been a destructive force in human lives. Sometimes, and closely related to the feeling of superiority, are false interpretations of scripture. These rise to such magnitude, though at variance with accepted, revealed doctrine, that they endanger the spiritual life of the individual. The various cults that arise, like mushrooms, from time to time, are but variations of this manner of destroying a testimony. They can always be recognized, for they are in opposition to some principle or regulation of the Church.

Most frequently, however, the loss of a testimony is due to finding fault with one's fellow believers, and with the leadership of the Church. Every action of bishop, stake president, or General Authority seems wrong, to such unfortunate people. Their vision distorts the world and all in it.

A dying testimony is easily recognized. The organizations and practices of the Church are ignored; the radio takes the place of the sacrament meeting; golf or motion pictures, the Sunday worship, the cup of coffee instead of the Word of Wisdom; the cold, selfish hand instead of helpfulness, charity for the poor, and the payment of tithing.

Soon, the testimony is gone, and the former possessor walks about, somewhat sour and discontented, and always in his heart, unhappy. He has lost his most precious possession, and has found nothing to replace it. He has lost inward freedom, the gift of obedience to law. (*John A. Widtsoe*, IE, May 1945, pp. 273, 280.)

(8E-4) *A sure way to bring an end to one's testimony.* Destructive criticism of the officers of the Church or its doctrine is sure to weaken and bring an eventual end to one's testimony if persisted in. (*Spencer W. Kimball*, CR, Oct. 1944, p. 45.)

(8E-5) *"That doesn't amount to anything."* I have never known in my life — and now I am eighty past — any man or woman to lose his or her faith in this Gospel, who once had a testimony of it and lived it.

I have seen men in high places start in by drinking tea and coffee, saying, "That doesn't amount to anything," then next using liquor, then next finding fault with the Authorities of the Church, and the first thing I knew they left the Church; but I have never known a person, man or woman, who attended his meetings, and partook of the spirit and inspiration that are present in the meetings of true, faithful Latter-day Saints, who has ever apostatized. (*Heber J. Grant*, CN, 10 Apr. 1937, p. 1.)

(8E-6) *He wondered why his spirit was dead.* At a distant stake conference one Sunday I was approached after the meeting by a young man whose face was familiar. He identified himself as a returned missionary whom I had met out in the world a few years ago. He said he had not attended the conference but had come at its conclusion, wanting to say hello. Our greetings were pleasant and revived some choice memories. I asked him about himself. He was in college, still single, and fairly miserable.

I asked him about his service in the Church, and the light in his eyes went out and a dull, disappointed face fashioned itself as he said, "I am not very active in the Church now. I don't feel the same as I used to feel in the mission field. What I used to think was a testimony has become something of a disillusionment. If there is a God, I am not sure any more. I must have been mistaken in my zeal and joy."

I looked him through and through and asked him some questions:

"What do you do in your leisure? What do you read? How much do you pray? What activity do you have? What are your associations?"

The answers were what I expected. He had turned loose his hold on the iron rod. He associated largely with unbelievers. He read, in addition to his college texts, works by atheists, apostates, and Bible critics. He had ceased to pray to his Heavenly Father. . . .

I asked him now, "How many times since your mission have you read the New Testament?"

"Not any time," was the answer.

"How many times have you read the Book of Mormon through?" The answer was, "None."

"How many chapters of scripture have you read? How many verses?"

Not one single time had he opened the sacred books. He had been reading negative and critical and faith-destroying things and wondered why he could not smile.

He never prayed any more, yet wondered why he felt so abandoned and so alone in a tough world. For a long time he had not partaken of the sacrament of the Lord's Supper, and he wondered why his spirit was dead.

Not a penny of tithing had he paid, and he wondered why the windows of heaven seemed closed and locked and barred to him. (*Spencer W. Kimball,* CR, Apr. 1972, pp. 27-28.)

(8E-7) *Those who think they have "outgrown" a testimony.* The few who claim, usually with a touch of self-praise, that they have outgrown Mormonism, really imply that they have developed beyond the gospel, miscalled Mormonism. That means, in turn, that they no longer need the truths and the principles of conduct which constitute the gospel. They have grown too large for the gospel, as for a suit of clothes, which is then cast off.

Such a position is untenable. They forget, in the words of Brigham Young, that "our religion is simply the truth." (*Discourses,* p. 2.) It has no other foundation. The doctrines of the gospel, such as the existence of God, the mission of Jesus the Christ, and the restoration of the gospel by Joseph Smith, the Prophet, are of an unchanging nature. They are eternal realities. Whatever the Church, the repository of the gospel, may undertake, must and does conform to truth, and rests upon that secure foundation.

Truth cannot be outgrown. No person is bigger than truth. It would be folly to try to make five out of two plus two, or to speak of outgrowing gravity, electricity, or the existence of the elements of nature; and a worse folly to do so in the equally real, spiritual realm. Truth may be accepted or rejected; but no further can man go in the unchanging kingdom. Whether we like it or not, truth remains the same; and our every act is affected by the foundation upon which we build our lives. . . .

The few who prattle about "outgrowing" Mormonism, have lost faith in the fundamental realities of the gospel. Their spiritual disorder roots in a lack of a sufficient doctrinal understanding. They are inclined to speak lightly of things which are not clear to their own minds. Earnest study and sincere practice pave the path to gospel comprehension. Only those who so do may speak with some authority on a gospel principle. Elder Orson F. Whitney tells of a woman friend, who had drifted away from the Church, because, as she said, she had graduated from its teachings. At a later gathering where the doctrines of the Church became the topic of conversation, she asked, "Elder Whitney, what is really the Mormon conception of God?" His answer was prompt: "Do I need to tell you that? You remarked a while ago that you had outgrown the doctrines of the Church; and the knowledge of God is the beginning of them all."

Too many people raise doubts in their own minds for lack of sufficient knowledge. That is why the Church, to the best of its ability, attempts in its organizations to teach gospel principles. That is why all members are advised to engage in regular, individual study of the gospel. To "outgrow" a system one does not properly understand, is a sad reflection upon the intelligence of the individual.

Others who say that they have "outgrown" the gospel, are merely seeking an excuse for their own behavior. They are the ones who are yielding to appetites and fashions contrary to gospel doctrine and injurious to their bodies and minds. Though ever so honest in their view of life, their dominating law is their own will, their self-interest, and their personal opinions. Even the moral law is frequently overshadowed by their willfulness. They resent the thought of being brought under any other dominion. The order of things must issue from them. They would abrogate the law of gravity when going uphill. They become easy faultfinders of persons and practices.

Therefore, for example, in defiance of the Word of Wisdom, their social group may begin the meal without a blessing, but with a highball. The cigaret follows. Nerve-stimulating beverages, such as coffee, tea, or cola drinks, are mere incidents at such a table. Other gospel principles are violated in a similar manner.

Faultfinding is much of the same order: The officials of the Church should or should not do that or that. It does not much matter what is being done. The bishop is under close scrutiny, the stake president likewise, and the general authorities most of all — and chiefly to discover the weaknesses and errors of the people involved. This group is seldom constructive.

If one raises a question concerning the propriety of yielding to fleshly appetites, or disregarding gospel requirements, the most common answer is that he is not "narrow," but "broad" enough to do as he pleases. That is, he is driven by a species of cowardice. This childish answer, of course, raises a smile in thoughtful people. People who "outgrow" the Church in such a manner are not to be taken seriously. Their soul-killing practices place them in danger of losing out in the battle between right and wrong.

Another group of "outgrowners" have become nearsighted, or have lost their sense of proportion, or have taken themselves too seriously. They are usually the student type, many of whom at one time may have known and lived the gospel well.

There is the young man who enters college. Soon he is overwhelmed with new facts, and unheard-of interpretations of the facts. His former convictions recede before the advancing wealth of knowledge, since he cannot of himself discriminate between factual and theoretical knowledge. Unless an honest and wise teacher rescues him, he may become lost in his inflated self-importance, and find himself with the "outgrown" ones. Pope had him in mind when he wrote: "Drink deep, or taste not the Pierian spring: There shallow draughts intoxicate the brain."

Then, there is the older man, who pursues the study of a subject, unremittingly, and to the exclusion of other human gains, into its minute and devious ramifications. He may even advance the boundaries of knowledge within his field. Soon, this special academic discipline rises to such proportions that he thinks and sees little else. It becomes the chief thing of consequence in the world and he himself often acquires, in his own mind, an importance which disdains learning, from any other source. His "specialty," with its problems and the opinions and theories of scholars, like a curtain, obscures his vision of the great world and its possessions. . . . Many who have "outgrown" Mormonism are merely perpetrating a fraud upon their senses. They cannot or will not view their "specialty" in its proper relationship and importance to the many things and thoughts and truths in the world of human beings. They are out of balance with the world.

These various groups who are subjected to the ever present temptation to depart from the truth, under the caption of "outgrowing" Mormonism, should examine, carefully, the processes which are leading them astray. They should do some hard, straight thinking. If they will do so earnestly, honestly, intelligently, and prayerfully, they will soon discover, to their full satisfaction, that no man can "outgrow" the gospel. They will learn that those who "outgrow" Mormonism are not happy. Happiness comes to those only who cling to truth.

It may be said further to those who are tempted, that protection from this type of error comes (1) when as much regular time is given to the study of the gospel as to the daily newspaper or the weekly and monthly magazines; (2) when, face to face with fleshly temptation, or faultfinding impulse, a man is sufficiently master of himself to say "no"; and (3) when he can place the affairs of his life in the order of their relative importance.

A man who does this will never "outgrow" the gospel, but ever grow in it.

Mormonism cannot be outgrown, because it encompasses all truth. (*John A. Widtsoe*, IE, Feb. 1945, pp. 85, 111.)

(8E-8) *Destroying their opportunities to grow.* Men and women who neglect to keep a radio communication with God are destroying, to a certain extent, their opportunities to grow in the knowledge and testimony of the divinity of this work. The Lord has said that it is our duty to supplicate him, and if we fail to do it we shall fail to grow as we otherwise would. . . . I say to you that of all my acquaintances I have never known of one who, having fulfilled the law, kept the commandments of God and supplicated him for his guidance, has ever lost the faith or the testimony of the divinity of this work in which we are engaged. (*Heber J. Grant*, IE, Aug. 1925, p. 931.)

(8E-9) *Spiritually cold and numb.* The following story I have used before, but because it seems to fit in this notch, may I repeat it?

"Dear Edgar:

"You told me of an experience you once had with a deer hunting companion in the High Uinta Mountains late one fall in bitter cold and stormy weather. Your companion had become lost, panicky, and exhausted from running over the mountainside. He had finally laid down under a pine tree, and by sheer luck you had come upon him before he froze to death. He was still conscious and could talk to you, but, in his numbed condition, claimed he was not cold at all. No amount of coaxing on your part could persuade him to get up and move around. He begged to be left alone, insisting he was perfectly comfortable and got sore when you dragged him to his feet and made him move. He really cussed you plenty, you said, when you at last in desperation picked up a stick and laid one or two across his back until he moved to get out of the reach of it. You had to drive him more than a mile like that, for every time you got sympathetic and eased up with the stick, he'd lie down again. Finally, however, you got him moving faster and faster to get out of the way of the stick and his blood warmed up and began circulating so when he could think clearly again he thanked you with tears in his eyes time and time again for using the stick and saving his life.

"I have the feeling since our conversation the other day that you, and hundreds of other good men like you, are in the same condition spiritually as your hunting companion was physically. You came home from your mission all enthused and for some reason you have grown cold. (I'll bet it's because of inactivity in the Church.) So cold you are numb, and can't think clearly in spiritual matters.

"More than likely you have gotten sore at your ward teachers because they would not leave you alone, and you've probably cussed (to their backs) your quorum president and your bishop because they would not go away and quit bothering you. Am I guessing correctly?"

One of the General Authorities has observed: "If we are not careful, we can be injured by the frostbite of frustration; we can be frozen in place by the chill of unmet expectations. To avoid this we must — just as we would with arctic coldness — keep moving, keep serving, and keep reaching out, so that our own immobility does not become our chief danger." (*Spencer W. Kimball*, EN, Dec. 1974, p. 4.)

(8E-10) *As long as you perform your duty.* How many of you who have received the testimony through the Spirit could become convinced that you are mistaken? You feel that the Lord has given you a knowledge for yourself; you know that this is the work of the Lord; you know that the Savior lives; you know that Joseph Smith was an inspired prophet of God, and as long as you perform your duty, and hold yourselves near to the Lord in prayer, that testimony cannot be taken from you. But if we neglect our duties, if we do things contrary to the will of the Lord, we can become dark. We can see in this hall at night when it is lighted up, but going out where it is dark we may remember what we have seen in the lighted hall, remember the light that lightened it; but outside, when we go into the land of the enemy, we cannot see our way, and we may even kick against the pricks; we may do that which we once knew to be wrong. Hence, let none of us forget how precious is the testimony of the Holy Spirit, to know that God lives, that his Son lives, and that his Son is coming again and will restore his kingdom upon the earth. (*Anthon H. Lund,* CR, Oct. 1919, p. 39.)

(8E-11) *Neglect of duty cuts off the channel of communication.* Today the radio discloses the fact that sound and other vibrations permeate the atmospheric realm surrounding the earth; but to hear these sounds one must get in *tune* with them by properly adjusting one's radio instrument. Analogously, so the Spirit of the Lord permeates all nature and influences it, and may inspire all human beings; but to receive the guidance, protection, and inspiration of the Holy Ghost one must put oneself "in tune" by obedience to eternal principles of conduct and by authoritative confirmation. To carry the analogy further: As the radio instrument may by excessive use or misuse become impaired and useless as an intermediary, so may a person by neglect of duty, by wrong-doing, or by sinful indulgence "cut off" the channel of communication between himself and the Holy Ghost. (*Charles A. Callis,* CN, 16 Sept. 1944, p. 13.)

F.   When Doubt Encroaches upon a Testimony

(8F-1) *Characteristics associated with a mature testimony.* Some people who claim to believe in the living prophets get confused over the statement of the Prophet Joseph Smith "that a prophet is a prophet only when he is acting as such." (DHC, vol. 5, p. 256.) Recently a young lady came seeking an interview. She wanted to know how she could tell when a prophet is speaking as a prophet. A few days later a perplexed young man came, questioning the recent restatement of the First Presidency of the Church concerning who can be given the priesthood.

This is not the place for me to repeat what I said to them. Suffice it to say that one with an informed testimony is never confused by such questions. He believes that everything said or done under the inspiration of the Holy Spirit carries with it the "witness of its authenticity." I would like to repeat that statement. (It is not mine; it is Brother Brigham Young's.) Everything that is said or done under the inspiration of the Holy Spirit carries with it the "witness of its authenticity." (Journal of Discourses, vol. 9, p. 149.)

When questions arise, one with a mature testimony of the gospel simply applies the test prescribed in Section 9 of the Doctrine and Covenants and finds out for himself. The Lord gave this test to Oliver Cowdery. "But, behold, I say unto you, that you must study it out in your mind; then you must ask me if it be right, and if it is right I will cause that your bosom shall burn within you; therefore, you shall feel that it is right. But if it be not right you shall have no such feelings, but you shall have a stupor of thought." (Doctrine and Covenants 9:8-9.)

With that test you can determine anything, if you are humble enough to get the inspiration of the Lord. If you are in harmony, you can ask the Lord if your answer is right. And if it is right, he will give you that burning in your soul that he promised Oliver Cowdery. Then you will know that it is right. (Marion G. Romney, BYU, 15 June 1971, pp. 1-2.)

(8F-2) When your testimony is waning. Young people, do not lose your testimony. You may discover sometimes that you are in doubt. I think we all have. You may sometimes wonder if your testimony is waning, but let that be a signal to you, let that be the time that you come to one of your brethren, one of your friends; that is the signal for you quickly to associate yourself with the Church and become very active in the Church, that is the time that you must confide in God your Eternal Father. (Thorpe B. Isaacson, CR, Oct. 1952, p. 66.)

9

RESPONSIBILITIES
AFTER OBTAINING
A TESTIMONY

A. Obedience: The True Measure of a Testimony

(9A-1) *Some people hear the words, some people understand.* I heard a Chinese proverb once that went something like this: The person who hears truth is not the equal of the person who understands truth, and the person who understands truth is not the equal of the person who loves truth. So it is with a testimony. Some people hear the words; some people understand. We're told even the devils believe, but it hasn't made any difference in their lives. Then there are those who love the truth, and when that happens their life changes. When that happens, they live the principles of the gospel of Jesus Christ even when they're on a desert island all by themselves, because they love the truth and they are committed to that principle of testimony so much that it has changed their lives.

Testimony is knowing that God lives and following him. Testimony is knowing that Jesus is the Christ and following him. Testimony is knowing that Joseph Smith was a true prophet and living the teachings he brought forth. Testimony is knowing that Spencer W. Kimball is a prophet of God and following his example. Testimony is knowing the Church is true and supporting it. Testimony is knowing the Book of Mormon is the word of God and living its teachings.

He that hears is not the equal of the person who understands, and the person who understands is not the equal of the person who loves the truth. (*Loren C. Dunn,* BYU, 1975, p. 70.)

(9A-2) *A testimony watered down by disobedience.* But how strong a voice can you raise? How strong a testimony can you bear? Your testimony is no stronger than your obedience. I wonder how much your testimony has been watered down by your disobedience even in little things here or there. But God expects that you will bear a mighty testimony to the world that he lives, that he has spoken in our day, that Jesus is the Christ, and that destruction will come upon the world unless we obey him and keep his commandments.

How strong is your testimony? I would have you know that your words alone are not enough. I would have you know that it is only your word supported by your righteous lives that can give testimony to the world in such sincere tones that men and women will pay attention to you. (*Mark E. Petersen,* CR, Oct. 1963, p. 122.)

(9A-3) *Ready and willing to do the will of the Lord.* A man who cannot sacrifice his own wishes, who cannot say in his heart, "Father, Thy will be done, not mine," is not a truly and thoroughly converted child of God; he is still, to some extent, in the grasp of error and in the shades of darkness that hover around the world, hiding God from the presence of mankind. Show me a man that is thoroughly converted to the principles of the Gospel, and who can truly say in his heart, "I know that the Gospel is true," and I will show you a man that when it comes to asking him to do that which God requires at his hands will have no question in his mind in relation to doing it; he will say, "Yes, I am ready and willing to do the will of God." (*Joseph F. Smith,* DW, 7 Jan. 1893, p. 67.)

(9A-4) *Because we know, we are bound.* Every one of you knows, and you can testify. That is one characteristic of the membership of this Church — we know we know! And therein lies the strength of the Church.

But because we know, brethren, we are bound. There are obligations imposed by our certain knowledge that we cannot logically escape. Obligations to do what? Keep the Lord's commandments is the answer. (*Joseph F. Merrill,* CR, Apr. 1944, p. 152.)

(9A-5) *Our lives must confirm our words.* The blessings of a testimony of Jesus that will lead to exaltation are reserved for those who *overcome* by faith, who are just men *made perfect,* and whose bodies become celestialized. Such blessings are not for those who claim to have a testimony and give only verbal expression of it. Our lives must confirm our words. When one's testimony has to do with convictions concerning conduct, then both consistency and honesty require that his conduct attest his belief. If one's declarations and his actions are at variance, then all who hear and see and note will disregard his protestations, be they ever so eloquent, and appraise him by what he does. (*Hugh B. Brown,* IN, Oct. 1959, p. 320.)

(9A-6) *The obligation to serve God.* We must remember, however, that we are not saved by virtue of a testimony alone. Testimony is only the beginning of real spiritual progress. A testimony carries with it the obligation to serve God and keep his commandments and always walk in the light of truth. No person in this church can honestly say that he has a true testimony of the gospel and yet neglect to keep God's commandments or fail to keep sacred the covenants and obligations he has entered into. A person advanced to an elevated testimony of truth and light should be above the weakness of the flesh to sin. (*Delbert L. Stapley,* BYU, 23 Mar. 1971, p. 4.)

(9A-7) *If we know the truth – we must do the right.* It will not do for us to be content and satisfied with the mere knowledge of that which is right. Knowing that which is right, we must go to and do the right thing, whatever it might be, whatever he requires of us. If we know the right, if we know the truth, we must abide by the right and in the truth, and we must do the right thing, always, under all circumstances, and never yield to the tempter or deviate from the right way, the straight and narrow path that leads back into the presence of God. (*Joseph F. Smith,* IE, Aug. 1906, p. 808.)

(9A-8) *The ability to live up to it.* It is a *glorious* thing to have a testimony of God's existence and of the divinity of Christ's Church. I do not know of anything more precious to you excepting life itself. With that testimony goes great responsibility — the ability to live up to it, to act in harmony with it. "He that knoweth to do good and doeth it not, to him it is sin." (*David O. McKay,* CN, 12 Sept. 1951, p. 2.)

(9A-9) *A truth is not a truth until you live it.* A truth of the gospel is not a truth until you live it. You do not really believe in tithing, and it is not a truth of the gospel to you until you pay it. The Word of Wisdom to you is not a truth of the gospel until you keep it. The Sabbath day is not a holy day unless you observe it. Fasting and paying fast offerings, consecrating your fast, is not a truth of the gospel unless you live it. Temple marriage does not mean anything to you unless you have a temple marriage. (*Harold B. Lee*, BYU, 19 Apr. 1961, p. 10.)

B. The Obligation to Make Your Testimony Known

(9B-1) *Every member has covenanted to be a witness.* Every elder, every member of the Church is a witness of the Lord. We are baptized, and part of the covenant of baptism says, "I covenant to stand as a witness of Christ at all times and in all places and under all circumstances, even until death." Every member of the Church has taken a solemn covenant to be a witness of the Lord Jesus Christ. Now that's the principle. What do we do about it in practice?

Every missionary that ever goes out is entitled to hear his mission president say in solemnity and in truth and with the Spirit accompanying, "I know this work is true. I know Jesus is the Lord. I know Joseph Smith is a prophet. I know Spencer W. Kimball holds the keys of the kingdom today."

Every student who goes to Sunday School class is entitled to hear the teacher of that class say, "I know this work is true." And so on through all the organizations. (*Bruce R. McConkie*, ACR, Feb. 1976 — Sydney, Australia, p. 21.)

(9B-2) *There is someone your testimony will appeal to.* Your testimony is different from any other testimony in the church. Your testimony is unique. Just as your combination of physical appearance and mental ability, social aptitudes, and spiritual capacity is unique, all of these contribute towards your testimony, and so your testimony is the product of your past effort, your various backgrounds, your experiences, and your sensitivity to things that are spiritual. And so no two testimonies are exactly alike, and the testimony that you have has a place in the Kingdom of God, and there is someone that your testimony will appeal to because your testimony is different than any other.

And so in the mission field we find thousands of missionaries. We find missionaries plowing the same ground that missionaries have plowed before. But here comes a missionary, in the eyes of the world probably much less qualified than others who have gone before, but there is a responsive chord as this missionary tells his story and bears his witness, because his testimony fits the person he's speaking with. (*Robert L. Simpson,* UA-CHD, 22 Aug. 1973 — Provo, Utah, pp. 3-4.)

(9B-3) *Three ways in which we bear testimony.* We bear testimony I suppose, in three ways. We can bear testimony in plain words; moved upon by the power of the Spirit, we can say that we know that such and such is the case. Secondly, we can bear testimony by teaching the doctrines of the kingdom, the principles that men must believe in order to inherit peace in this life and have eternal reward in the life to come. In section 76 the record says that "the record which we bear is the fulness of the gospel of Jesus Christ." (Doctrine and Covenants 76:14.) So we bear testimony, secondly, when we teach the doctrines of the gospel which we have and the world does not have. And then thirdly, we bear testimony of the divinity of the work that we are engaged in when we live in harmony with its standards so that the light of the gospel goes forth from us to other people so that they, seeing our good works, will be led to glorify our Father who is in heaven. (*Bruce R. McConkie,* ACR, Feb. 1976 — Sydney, Australia, p. 17.)

(9B-4) *One cannot thereafter remain passive.* When one obtains a living, vital witness, a knowledge that "God is his Father, that Jesus is the Christ, that men are brothers, that life is a mission and not a career" (Elder Stephen L Richards), he is born again. He has acquired the necessary motivating force which changes his life. Hate, lust, greed, and all evil impulses leave him. His whole desire is for good.

One who gains this witness cannot thereafter remain passive. He acquires something of the spirit of Peter and John who, upon being threatened by Annas the high priest and his associates "not to speak at all nor teach in the name of Jesus . . . answered and said unto them, Whether it be right in the sight of God to hearken unto you more than unto God, judge ye. For we cannot but speak the things which we have seen and heard." (Acts 4:18-20.) (*Marion G. Romney,* CN, 17 July 1943, p. 8.)

(9B-5) *Obligation to make testimony known.* We are told in . . . [the] . . . Doctrine of Covenants that this is a day of warning, and not of many words, when every man who receiveth the light and truth should warn his neighbor. The trouble is, we do not do this. We feel that unless we are specifically called to labor in one of the missionary fields we have not the right to make known our testimony of the Gospel of the Lord Jesus Christ. This is a mistake. Everyone who has received a testimony that this work is of God is at perfect liberty to bear that testimony to his or her neighbors; and indeed, I feel that we will come under some degree of condemnation before God if we fail to do this. If we have received the pearl of great price, let us not hug it to ourselves and say that we do not want others to receive it, for fear it would diminish our joy and satisfaction to see them enjoying a like blessing. This is not the spirit of the Gospel. Every member of the Church of Christ, whether male or female, ought to be continually anxious that a knowledge of the Gospel shall be spread to every creature upon the earth. We are as a light set upon a hill, a beacon to the world; and we ought not to hide this light, but strive to let it so shine that people seeing our good works may be led to glorify God. This is the desire that should prompt us in our lives. We would then seek after eternal riches, even the bringing about of the salvation of the souls of men, more than we do other things. (*Abraham O. Woodruff*, CR, Apr. 1902, p. 31.)

(9B-6) *Be not miserly in your feelings.* A man who wishes to receive light and knowledge, to increase in the faith of the Holy Gospel, and to grow in the knowledge of the truth as it is in Jesus Christ, will find that when he imparts knowledge to others he will also grow and increase. Be not miserly in your feelings, but get knowledge and understanding by freely imparting it to others, and be not like a man who selfishly hoards his gold; for that man will not thus increase upon the amount, but will become contracted in his views and feelings. So the man who will not impart freely of the knowledge he has received, will become so contracted in his mind that he cannot receive truth when it is presented to him. Wherever you see an opportunity to do good, do it, for that is the way to increase and grow in the knowledge of the truth. (*Brigham Young,* DW, 9 May 1855, p. 68.)

C. Being Valiant in the Testimony of Jesus

(9C-1) *Lukewarm members of the Church are not valiant.* It is not enough to have a testimony. You want to know what happens to people who have a testimony, who do not work at it? Read it in the vision of the degrees of glory (Doctrine and Covenants 76); it is talking about the terrestrial kingdom. And it says that those who are not valiant in the testimony of Jesus, obtain not the crown over the kingdom of our God. That means members of the Church who are lukewarm. They are members of the Church who manage to get in tune on occasions, so that a flash of lightning comes to them, and they know in their hearts that the work is true. Maybe they work at it for a while. Maybe they go on a mission for a couple of years and then they fall away. They get into the state where they know the work is true, but they are not valiant. They do not endure in righteousness to the end.

There are lots of people in the Church who know this work is true who do not do very much about it. But if you backed them into a corner and began to condemn the Church, they would stand up in wrath and ire and defend the kingdom. This is all to their credit and all to their advantage. But they go fishing; that is, they go off after the things of the world instead of putting first in their lives the things of God's kingdom, the things of righteousness. And hence they are lukewarm, they are not valiant. (*Bruce R. McConkie*, BYU, 11 Feb. 1968, pp. 12-13.)

(9C-2) *To be valiant in the testimony of Jesus is to* . . . Members of the Church who have testimonies and who live clean and upright lives, but who are not courageous and valiant, do not gain the celestial kingdom. Theirs is a terrestrial inheritance. Of them the revelation says, "These are they who are not valiant in the testimony of Jesus; wherefore, they obtain not the crown over the kingdom of our God." (Doctrine and Covenants 76:79.)

As Jesus said, "No man, having put his hand to the plough, and looking back, is fit for the kingdom of God" (Luke 9:62). . . .

Now, what does it mean to be valiant in the testimony of Jesus?

It is to be courageous and bold; to use all our strength, energy, and ability in the warfare with the world; to fight the good fight of faith. "Be strong and of a good courage," the Lord commanded Joshua, and then specified that this strength and courage consisted of meditating upon and observing to do all that is written in the law of the Lord. (See Joshua 1:6-9.) The great cornerstone of valiance in the cause of righteousness is obedience to the whole law of the whole gospel.

To be valiant in the testimony of Jesus is to "come unto Christ, and be perfected in him"; it is to deny ourselves "of all ungodliness," and "love God" with all our "might, mind and strength." (Moroni 10:32.)

To be valiant in the testimony of Jesus is to believe in Christ and his gospel with unshakable conviction. It is to know of the verity and divinity of the Lord's work on earth.

But this is not all. It is more than believing and knowing. We must be doers of the word and not hearers only. It is more than lip service; it is not simply confessing with the mouth the divine Sonship of the Savior. It is obedience and conformity and personal righteousness. "Not every one that saith unto me, Lord, Lord, shall enter into the kingdom of heaven; but he that doeth the will of my Father which is in heaven." (Matthew 7:21.) (*Bruce R. McConkie*, CR, Oct. 1974, pp. 44-46.)

(9C-3) *A testimony does not guarantee the celestial kingdom.* As we seek to develop and strengthen these testimonies, we must always rely on the Lord and place our highest priority on spiritual values. We must not forget, however, that a testimony does not, in and of itself, guarantee that we will inherit the celestial kingdom. We might know the gospel is true, but unless we are valiant, live righteous lives, and work to build the kingdom here on earth, we will not inherit celestial glory. (*O. Leslie Stone*, CR, Apr. 1975, p. 11.)

D.   Testimony and Conversion Are Not Necessarily the Same

(9D-1) *The process of conversion.* Now I say all of us, hopefully, do have testimonies. All of us are not converted. But all of us ought to be in the process of becoming converted. . . . With most people, conversion is a process; and it goes step by step, degree by degree, level by level, from a lower state to a higher, from grace to grace, until the time that the individual is wholly turned to the cause of righteousness. Now this means that an individual overcomes one sin today and another sin tomorrow. He perfects his life in one field now, and in another field later on. And the conversion process goes on, until it is completed, until we become, literally, as the Book of Mormon says, saints of God instead of natural men. This is the language that the angel told King Benjamin, as you know. Read the third chapter of the Book of Mosiah.

Well, now what we are striving to do is to be converted. It is not enough to have a testimony. (*Bruce R. McConkie*, BYU, 11 Feb. 1968, p. 12.)

(9D-2) *A testimony and faith are not always synonymous.* Testimony is vitally important *but* men are not saved by virtue of their testimony alone, although it is the beginning of real spiritual progress.

It is a common error to feel that testimony means full conversion. We many times equate testimony with a man's faith. We say, "He has great faith," meaning that he has a strong testimony, or we say, "he has a strong testimony," meaning that he has great faith. However, I don't believe the two are always synonymous. Faith is based on knowledge; it is a hope in that which is not seen which is true. (See Alma 32:21.) Testimony is revealed knowledge. . . .

Peter had a testimony that Jesus is the Christ, which he bore, and it surely came from the Lord, for the Master said, ". . . flesh and blood hath not revealed it unto thee, but my Father which is in heaven." (Matthew 16:17.) It is very doubtful that Peter was at that time converted, because he could not admit that he knew the Lord Jesus Christ when he felt his own life was in danger. Later the Master confirmed that Peter lacked conversion when, just before going to his agony and death on the cross, he said to Peter, ". . . when thou art converted, strengthen thy brethren." (Luke 22:32.) Peter's testimony or knowledge that Jesus was the Christ did not "save" him from denying the Master — probably because he was not converted. He did not follow the Lord at the peril of his own life.

When we are converted, we sustain and follow the Lord's anointed servants; we find ourselves in agreement with them. This is one of the real marks of conversion. Many men with testimonies have been unable to do this. In this dispensation, to name a few, Martin Harris, David Whitmer, and Oliver Cowdery (the Three Witnesses to the Book of Mormon) and Thomas B. Marsh (the first president of the Quorum of the Twelve) had this very problem. They refused to sustain the Lord's anointed servant, and it led to their expulsion from his church.

Conversion implies a change; as King Benjamin says, it means putting "off the natural man," which is selfish, conceited, impatient, intemperate, disobedient, and rebellious, so that a person becomes "a saint through the atonement of Christ the Lord." This would mean becoming even "as a child, submissive, meek, humble, patient, full of love, willing to submit to all things which the Lord seeth fit to inflict upon him, even as a child doth submit to his father." (Mosiah 3:19.)

In order to emphasize this particular point, Jesus said, "Not [he] that saith . . . Lord, Lord, [will be saved] but he that doeth the will of my Father which is in heaven." (Matthew 7:21.)

Jesus was committed completely to doing the will of his Father, and he was unequivocal in his counsel to us that we follow him in doing the will of the Father. Those who are truly converted desire to do the will of the Father. . . .

Testimony won't save us, but testimony coupled with faith and conversion, which includes staying power, which is endurance, will exalt us. (*Hartman Rector, Jr.*, CR, Apr. 1974, pp. 159-161.)

(9D-3) *Measure of true conversion: into your heart like fire.* I listened to an excerpt of a testimony of a man who was a member of the Twelve and of whom President Grant had said that he never knew a man who had a greater gift of prophecy than did this man. There was put in my hands a quotation from a sermon that he had delivered some fifty years before, which proved to be the last sermon he had ever delivered as a member of the Twelve. Before another conference, he was dropped from the Council of the Twelve and subsequently left the Church. This is what he said, in that last sermon: "That person is not truly converted unless he sees the power of God resting upon the leaders of this Church and it goes down into his heart like fire." And I repeat that to you here today. The measure of your true conversion and whether or not you hold fast to those ideals is whether or not you are so living that you see the power of God resting upon the leaders of this Church and that testimony goes down into your heart like fire. (*Harold B. Lee*, BYU, 1973, p. 90.)

(9D-4) *There is a difference between being convinced and converted.* Many of you who now hear my witness are convinced that I am speaking the truth! I ask, however, for more than conviction — I ask for conversion. There is a great difference between a person who is convinced and one who is converted. We have a well-known saying, "A man convinced against his will is of the same opinion still." The very definition of the word "convince" tells us that to convince is "to overwhelm with arguments and reasons," whereas to convert is "to cause a person to change his character." Therefore, I will not presume to convince you, but would be grateful if you would convert yourselves to the divinity of

Jesus Christ. If I am to assist you in this conversion, I must speak not to your minds, but to your hearts. No logic nor arguments, however brilliant, can convert you, but a word spoken in sincerity to your hearts may touch a chord of sympathy which may help in your conversion. . . .

Know this that any testimony we have, any faith we possess, must be tested to see if it is real. If faith is nothing more than conviction, it will fail. If you are *only* convinced, your faith will fail in a time of crisis. Oliver Cowdery, for instance, had the same blessings and experiences as Joseph Smith. He was ordained of John the Baptist and later by Peter, James and John. He heard the voice of God; he saw the original golden plates of the Book of Mormon. No man was ever more convinced than he, for even in the face of ridicule, and regardless of prestige or position, he affirmed that the testimony he previously gave was true. Yet, he failed when the test of strength came. . . .

The whole *purpose* of life is to test us to see if we have caught the real *meaning* of divinity. When the trial of faith comes with its doubts and cares and worries, one must be clothed with the whole armor of God. Unless one has accepted this gospel of Jesus Christ without reserve and without mental reservations as the *only* way of life, that great happiness cannot come to man. (*Theodore M. Burton*, BYU, 6 Oct. 1964, pp. 2, 7.)

10
BEARING YOUR TESTIMONY

A. Expressing Yourself in a Proper Manner

(10A-1) *Don't preach a sermon.* Now, you are going to give your testimonies this afternoon. I hope that you'll just open your hearts and let us look inside . . . will you? Just open them up wide and turn on the lights and let us see your hearts . . . how you feel. A testimony is not an exhortation; a testimony is not a sermon; none of you are here to exhort the rest. You are here to bear your own witness. It is amazing what you can say in thirty seconds by way of testimony, or in sixty seconds, or one hundred and twenty, or two hundred and forty, or whatever time you are given, if you confine yourselves to testimony. We'd like to know how you feel. (*Spencer W. Kimball*, UA-CHD, 2 Jan. 1959 — Los Angeles, California, p. 9.)

(10A-2) *Just tell how you feel.* God bless you, brethren and sisters, as you enter now into this testimony bearing. Do not exhort each other, that is not a testimony. Do not tell others how to live. Just tell how you feel inside. That is the testimony. The moment you begin preaching to others, your testimony ended. Just tell us how you feel, what your mind and heart and every fiber of your body tells you. (*Spencer W. Kimball*, UA-CHD, 15 Jan. 1962 — Berlin, Germany, p. 5.)

(10A-3) *Statements of public thanks.* Bearing testimony has to do with bearing witness to that which we know to be true. Much of what we call testimony bearing is not really testimony at all — it is a statement or expression of public thanks. It is good to be thankful, but public thanks is not testimony. Testimony comes from the Holy Ghost. (*Hartman Rector, Jr.,* CR, Apr. 1974, p. 159.)

(10A-4) *Something more than a passing reference.* I would hope that as Latter-day Saints we can strengthen each other in the way which the Lord provided, by bearing our testimonies often — at church meetings, at the end of gospel classes, even at fast and testimony meetings. We should renew our efforts to actually express our testimonies and give something more than a passing reference to the truthfulness of the gospel. With the bearing of testimony comes the spirit of testimony, and all are edified. (*Loren C. Dunn,* CR, Oct. 1972, p. 97.)

(10A-5) *Crying while bearing testimony.* You don't have to cry about the gospel to have a testimony! Many times we think that we don't have a testimony unless a few tears flow. Nothing could be further from the truth. It is not necessary or needful for a person to have tears streaming down their face to have a testimony of the gospel.

I remember a missionary once who used to cry so badly when he bore his testimony that I finally just told him, "Elder, I think you are making a demonstration of yourself. Why don't you try bearing your testimony without crying. You don't have to shed tears." I know that there are occasions when our hearts are close to the surface, and tears come. I've seen that in President McKay. But, I tell you, the serenity of the gospel of Jesus Christ does not depend upon emotionalism to bring forth a testimony. These things are firmly fixed under the power of the spirit. They don't require a physical emotionalism to demonstrate testimony because they are born of a solid conviction by the power of truth! I found out with this missionary that as a young man he had borne his testimony for the first time and it had caused him to cry and everyone had come up and told him what a wonderful testimony it was. That was the springboard. From then on he cried every time he bore his testimony, so people would come up and say what a wonderful testimony he had.

I went to a meeting with Spencer W. Kimball and a man got up and bore his testimony and he cried all the way through it. After the meeting, Brother Kimball called him over and said, "Brother, I wish you'd stop crying when you bear your testimony. You don't have to do that to tell people that you love the Lord."

I felt embarrassed for another missionary who bore his testimony and said, "If you'll pardon me, I'm overcome" and he really wept, and when he got through, Brother Bennion really took him apart. He wasn't trying to be unkind to the missionary, but sometimes you can be misled by over-emotionalism, which is merely a surging of the blood. It is not a conviction! I think we ought to bear our testimonies without tears, and stand strong and honorably before our fellow men and tell them the truth, born of the spirit that comes to us. Now I know that isn't always easy, and I know I have had to struggle many times to keep back the tears, and I don't think we ought to fight that either. I hope you understand what I mean, but there are people who can bring tears pretty fast, and sometimes it is an indication of a lack of sincerity. (*Alvin R. Dyer*, UA-CHD, 25 Mar. 1961 — Berlin, Germany, pp. 12-13.)

(10A-6) *Testimony not to be used to "fill up time."* The sanctity of a true testimony should inspire a thoughtful care as to its use. That testimony is not to be forced upon everybody, nor is it to be proclaimed at large from the housetop. It is not to be voiced merely to "fill up the time" in a public meeting; far less to excuse or disguise the speaker's poverty of thought or ignorance of the truth he is called to expound.

There are many in our Church who seem to regard the proclaiming of their conviction regarding the truth of the Gospel, the bearing of their testimony — as fully meeting all requirements of any speaker called to address the people in worshiping assemblies, on any and every occasion. That such a conception is false a little thought will show. How plainly inconsistent is it to boldly declare that the Gospel we teach is true, and yet be inexcusably ignorant as to the principles and precepts of the Gospel itself. A testimony of the truth enshrined in the honest soul as a precious gift from God, does not give to its owner a knowledge of the scriptures, or an understanding of the plan of salvation. The possession of such a testimony should of itself be an effective incentive to study, research, and prayerful investigation; it is a light to the feet that tread the path of wisdom, not a cloak to hide the ignorance due to sloth. (*Joseph F. Smith*, JI, 1 Aug. 1906, p. 465.)

B.   Use of the Words "I Know" in a Testimony

(10B-1) *Don't you ever worry about triteness.* Some of our good people get so terrified at triteness that they try to get clear around and away from their testimonies by getting out on the fringes that they won't become trite. Don't you ever worry about triteness in testimony. When the President of the Church bears his testimony, his eyes sparkle and his voice is resonant, but he says, "I know that Joseph Smith was called of God, a divine representative. I know that Jesus is the Christ, the Son of the living God." You see, the same thing that everyone of you said. That is testimony. (*Spencer W. Kimball,* UA-CHD, 2 Jan. 1959 — Los Angeles, California, pp. 16-17.)

(10B-2) *There are no words like "I know."* I know it is true. Because that word, those few words have been said a billion times by millions of people does not make it trite. It will never be worn out. I feel sorry for people who try to couch it in other words because there are no words like "I know." There are no words which express the deep feelings which can come from the human heart like "I know." (*Spencer W. Kimball,* UA-CHD, 15 Jan. 1962 — Berlin, Germany, p. 5.)

(10B-3) *Even a counterfeit person could say "I know."* "No man can say that Jesus is the Lord, but by the Holy Ghost," so declared Paul to the Corinthians two thousand years ago. (1 Corinthians 12:3.) The Prophet Joseph corrected one word in that quotation. Instead of "no man can *say,*" the Prophet Joseph declared that the wording should be by proper interpretation, "no man can *know* that Jesus is the Lord, but by the Holy Ghost." I suppose that anybody could *say* it, even a counterfeit person, but only one that is convinced can really *know* it and *say* it with conviction. (*Robert L. Simpson,* BYU, 18 Oct. 1966, p. 3.)

C.   Use of Sacred Experiences in a Testimony

(10C-1) *Not for the Church as a whole.* Revelations of divine manifestations for the comfort of individuals may be received by every worthy member of the Church. In that respect all faithful members of the Church are equal. Such manifestations most commonly guide the recipients to the solution of personal problems; though, frequently, they open the mind to a clearer comprehension of the Lord's vast plan of salvation. They are cherished possessions, and should be valued, of those who receive them. In their very nature they are sacred and should be so treated. If a person who has received such a manifestation by dream, vision, or otherwise, feels impressed to relate it beyond his immediate family circle, he should present it to his bishop, but not beyond. The bishop, then, may decide upon its further use, if any, or may submit it to those of higher authority for action. The gift was a personal one; not for the Church as a whole; and the recipient is under obligation, in harmony with the established order, not to broadcast it over the Church.

It is unwisdom, therefore, for those who have received such manifestations to send copies to others, to relate them by word of mouth in diverse places, and otherwise to scatter abroad a personal, sacred experience. There are times and places where testimony may be borne of our knowledge that the restored gospel is of the Lord, and of the goodness of the Lord to us, and when we may present evidence of our faith. It would be well to remember that the Lord Jesus Christ, while on earth, usually instructed those whom He had healed or otherwise blessed, that they should not tell others of the occurrence. Some things are done for the public good, others for private welfare. (*John A. Widtsoe,* IE, Sept. 1940, pp. 545, 575.)

(10C-2) *They have their own reward.* Some people have had a unique testimony, and to draw attention they go around repeating it again and again everywhere they go. Some have even published them and had them broadcast over the Church. They tell of dreams, and of administrations when they have been healed. Well, they have their reward. These are wonderful blessings, but why, why do they think they have to publicize it all over the Church? (*Harold B. Lee,* BYU, 19 Apr. 1961, p. 9.)

D.   Testimony Meetings

(10D-1) *Testimony meetings are necessary at all levels.* Now this testimony bearing . . . is not something we do just in the missions, we do it at home in our gatherings. . . . We have testimonies all through the Church.

When we get a group of presidents of missions together, we bear our testimonies and when members get together in little groups almost anywhere, they formally or informally bear their testimonies.

At home we bear testimonies, we of the Twelve. The eighteen and a half years I have been in the Twelve, we have been holding a quarterly testimony meeting. We go to the Temple early in the morning, the twelve of us, or as many as are not too far away from headquarters. We often travel hundreds of miles to get back to this testimony meeting, but if we are away around the world, sometimes we must miss it. But as many of us as possible meet in our own room up on the fourth floor. Here is a room in which there are twelve old leather-covered chairs. They are very old. I think they have been occupied by apostles for half a century at least. The leather is wearing, but they are still comfortable old chairs. They are in a semi-circle. We have our clerk there. President Smith sits at one end and the youngest member sits at the other. We sit in horse-shoe fashion. We sing. Brother Lee plays the organ or he leads the singing and I play the organ. We have a little pump organ which we pump with our feet. We pray very earnestly for the Spirit of the Lord to be with us and then we hear the minutes of our last meeting in great detail. The minutes take fifteen or twenty minutes to read. . . . Those minutes are thrilling. We hear again the testimonies we heard three months ago from the brethren. . . .

We have had the sacrament, of course, and we are fasting. Two of us administer to it, and pass the sacrament to each other. And then the testimonies begin. We spend three or four hours, just the twelve of us, bearing testimony to each other. I mention this so you may know this is basic and is an important part of the Church program. If the Twelve Apostles need to bear testimony to each other to express themselves and speak their gratitude to the Lord, then the missionaries may need it too, to sustain and lift and inspire them, and to keep the fires burning. We sing again, and pray, and go back to our regular duties.

Now, we have another testimony meeting every six months on the Thursday preceding General Conference. All of the General Authorities are there. . . . We assemble in the room of the Presidency and the Twelve in the temple. At the top is a chair in which the President sits. Never does anyone sit in that chair, except the Prophet of the Lord. Even though his counselors conduct the meeting when he is gone, always they sit in their own chairs. . . .

Now in this special testimony meeting, the others are there too, and they sit around in front of us on special seats that are brought in for this occasion only. The sacrament is administered by two of the brethren (we are fasting), generally two of the Twelve. Then we have our testimonies. The Patriarch, one of the Bishopric, one of the Seventies, one of the Assistants, one or more of the Twelve, and all three of the Presidency bear their testimonies. It is a glorious experience to have it all capped by the testimony of the Prophet of the Lord. To hear him stand there and say, "I know it is true, I know the Lord is responding. He is revealing His mind and will to us." I tell you that is an experience to remember.

I mention this so you do not think that testimony bearing is some little thing that is incidental to the mission only. This is the Church program. It is powerful and mighty. Can you see how important the testimony is? It is the lifeblood of the organization of the Church. (*Spencer W. Kimball*, UA-CHD, 15 Jan. 1962 — Berlin, Germany, pp. 1-3.)

(10D-2) *If you are bored there is something the matter with you.* These testimony meetings are the best meetings in the Ward in the whole month, if you have the spirit. If you are bored at a testimony meeting there is something the matter with you, and not with the other people. You can get up and bear your testimony and it is the best meeting in the month; but if you sit there and count the grammatical errors and laugh at the man who can't speak good English, you'll be bored, and on that board you'll slip right out of the Kingdom. Don't forget it! Any one of you could apostatize! Tomorrow you could be an excommunicant! Don't you forget it! You can lose your testimony! (*Spencer W. Kimball*, UA-CHD, 2 Jan. 1959 — Los Angeles, California, pp. 15-16.)

(10D-3) *Cultivation of feelings of gratitude.* Testimony-bearing should have a strong educational influence upon the feelings and lives of the children, and it is intended to cultivate within them feelings of thankfulness and appreciation for the blessings they enjoy. The Spirit of God may work within the life of a child and make the child realize and know that this is the work of God. The child knows it rather because of the Spirit than because of some physical manifestation which he may have witnessed. Our testimony meetings, then should have as one of their aims the cultivation of the children's feelings of gratitude not only toward God, but toward their parents, teachers, and neighbors. It is advisable, therefore, to cultivate as far as possible their appreciation for the blessings they enjoy. . . .

Testimony bearing is chiefly for the benefit of those who bear the testimony, in that their gratitude and appreciation are deepened. Testimony bearing is not the accumulation of arguments or evidences solely for the satisfaction and testimony of others. Let the testimonies then of the young people include the training of their feelings by way of making them more appreciative and more thankful for the blessings they enjoy, and the children should be made to understand what these blessings are and how they come to them. It is an excellent way to make people helpful and thankful to others, by first making them thankful to God. (*Joseph F. Smith*, JI, 15 Apr. 1903, pp. 245-246.)

(10D-4) *I feel that the Lord is not pleased.* We as a people have the privilege of fasting once a month, and donating that which we otherwise would consume for the benefit of the poor and the needy among us. This is pretty generally observed by the Latter-day Saints. But in our fast meetings I have felt sometimes as though we did not always appreciate the blessings that we enjoy. I have attended fast meetings where the Bishops have felt very ill at ease on account of the people not responding to the invitation to bear their testimony. There seems to be too much backwardness on the part of the Saints in taking advantage of this blessing when it is placed within their reach; and some of those who do arise to testify of the goodness of God are looked upon as putting themselves forward a little too much. . . . I feel that it is a mistake for us to go to fast meetings, and allow the time to pass without utilizing it in the manner designated of the Lord; and I know that in failing to do our duty in this regard we are not obedient to the promptings of the Spirit of God. The Saints should heed the promptings of the Spirit at all times; for if they do not the voice of the Spirit becomes less distinct within them and they do not experience it in such power as it comes to them when they are obedient to its teachings. The Apostles and Elders in the Church of Christ, in this day as in former days, have had as their especial guide the whisperings of the "still small voice" within them. Why, therefore, should we not be obedient to this Spirit when it prompts us in our fast meetings to bear testimony of the goodness of God to us?

... Not that we should give way to any great demonstration; that is not the proper thing; but we should enjoy the peaceful influence of the Spirit of God, and there should never be one, two or five minutes wasted in our fast meetings. You, no doubt, have all experienced a difference in attending fast meetings. Sometimes the people will respond readily; there is a rich outpouring of the Spirit of God; our faith is increased, and we feel to thank the Lord for the privilege of being present. At other times the people show reluctance in responding and telling what God has done for them; then we go home feeling that we have not taken advantage of our opportunities and have not listened to the promptings of the Spirit. (*Abraham O. Woodruff, CR, Apr. 1901, pp. 11-12.*)

(10D-5) *No one has had too many opportunities.* Now when you [missionaries] go home, don't you sit there in your Sacrament Fast Meeting and cheat yourself and say to yourself, "I guess I won't bear my testimony today. I guess that wouldn't be fair to these other members because I have had so many opportunities." *You bear your testimony every Testimony Day and every Testimony Meeting that you are in. Every one!* And one minute is long enough to bear it, as we have proven today with one hundred and fifty witnesses. One minute, two minutes ... *plenty* of time! (*Spencer W. Kimball, UA-CHD, 2 Jan. 1959 — Los Angeles, California, p. 15.*)

(10D-6) *A source of help and encouragement.* In the organized wards of the Church, testimony meetings are provided for. These gatherings are characterized by the voluntary expression of individual testimony regarding the restored Gospel and as to the divine grace and goodness shown in personal experience of blessings received. In meetings of this kind, testimony-bearing is in place, and operates as a source of help and encouragement to the participants. (*Joseph F. Smith, JI, 1 Aug. 1906, p. 465.*)

(10D-7) *One does not need perpetual reasons for reentry.* Sometimes in a fast and testimony meeting one hears reported an event or instance which by itself is not persuasive or even impressive to others. Care must be taken by the listener, however, to distinguish between the person's basic and original conversion and what is often added evidence or a report of transitory blessings.

When we first cross the border of belief and enter the territory of testimony, that is a highly significant moment. We come through, as it were, a port of entry. The Spirit has borne witness to us that Jesus is the Christ, that God lives, that other truths related to these are accepted by us. Our later experiences do not really represent the recrossing of that border again and again. One does not need perpetual reasons for reentry.

These later reports are most often a result of — not solely a reason for — believing. They are experiences to be shared gratefully as a result of one's adventures further inland in the second estate which corroborate one's convictions. These often reflect spiritual maturity rather than the recrossing of the borders of belief time and again; they are like sending exclaiming postcards which reflect progress in the journey in an increasingly celestial countryside. (*Neal A. Maxwell*, DD, p. 51.)

11

HELPING OTHERS TO GAIN A TESTIMONY

A. A Testimony May Not Be Bequeathed to Another

(11A-1) *No man can convert another.* That testimony once given you is yours. You can't give it away. You can't get rid of it. There are some things in this world, given of God, that we cannot impart, cannot dispossess ourselves of, liberal though we may be.

How many a man who perhaps through effort and study and sacrifice has become learned in a profession, would like, if he could, to give part of his skill to somebody else, bequeath it, perhaps. What great musician has ever yet been able to make an effective will leaving his skill as a bequest to his son? The only way that a son can acquire the knowledge and the skill that his father had or knowledge and skill like unto it, is to do as his father did by effort and by sacrifice, and then the skill so found is his. We can't give these things away, but thanks be unto God we can help one another. We can show those who would become possessors of the testimony such as we have, just how and where to get one for themselves; we can help them. No man can convert another, but it is given unto man by earnest effort to put others on the road to conversion, to lead them along in part, and to show them how they may obtain that priceless knowledge direct from the divine source. (*James E. Talmage*, MS, 28 Dec. 1972, p. 819.)

(11A-2) *It has to come from your own searching.* Now when our missionaries go out, we say to those among whom they labor, "We are not asking you to join the Church just to put your name on the records. That is not our concern. We come to you offering you the greatest gift the world can give, the gift of the kingdom of God. This is here for you if you will only accept and believe." Now that is our challenge to the world. "We can teach you the doctrines of the Church of Jesus Christ and bear testimony of the divinity of the work, but the witness of the truth of what we teach has to come from your own searching."

We say to our people whom we teach, "Now, you ask the Lord. Study, work, and pray." (*Harold B. Lee,* ACR, Aug. 1972 — Mexico City, Mexico, pp. 117-118.)

(11A-3) *Impossible for me to know for you.* It is impossible for me to know for you, or for any man to know for me. The Spirit of God does not reveal to you the Gospel, or bear witness to you of the Father, for me. I cannot save you; you cannot save me. No man can be a savior in this sense to any other man. Yet the man who has the testimony of the Spirit in his heart and who has a knowledge of the first principles of the Gospel may declare them to another, and by so declaring another soul may be convinced of the truth and be led to embrace it for himself. But it is *his* obedience to the Gospel and *his* own works of righteousness which save him, and not that of the man that bears testimony to him. It is only in this way that the man can be saved. (*Joseph F. Smith,* DW, 28 July 1894, p. 162.)

(11A-4) *He can touch your understanding: I cannot.* We have derived this knowledge from the Lord, not from man. Man cannot give this knowledge. I may tell you what I know, but that is not knowledge to you. If I have learned something through prayer, supplication, and perseverance in seeking to know the truth, and I tell it to you, it will not be knowledge unto you. I can tell you how you obtain it, but I cannot give it to you. If we receive this knowledge it must come from the Lord. He can touch your understandings and your spirits, so that you shall comprehend perfectly and not be mistaken. But I cannot do that. You can obtain this knowledge through repentance, humility, and seeking the Lord with full purpose of heart until you find Him. He is not afar off. It is not difficult to approach Him, if we will only do it with a broken heart and contrite spirit, as did Nephi of old. This is the way in which Joseph Smith, in his boyhood, approached Him. (*Joseph F. Smith*, CR, Oct. 1899, p. 71.)

(11A-5) *No testimonies to sell.* Every member of this Church stands upon his own feet, upon his own testimony, upon his own conviction that this is the Church of Jesus Christ. He cannot receive that testimony from any other man. No president, no apostle, no patriarch, no bishop, no officer in the Church has any testimonies to sell, nor any assurances of the divinity of this work to give as a personal possession to anybody else. (*James E. Talmage*, CR, Apr. 1920, p. 104.)

(11A-6) *One cannot give his testimony to another.* The individual testimony is a personal possession. One cannot give his testimony to another, yet he is able to aid his earnest brother in gaining a true testimony for himself. The over-zealous missionary may be influenced by the misleading thought that the bearing of his testimony to those who have not before heard the Gospel message, is to convince or condemn, as the hearers accept or reject. The elder is sent into the field to preach the Gospel — the good news of its restoration to earth, showing by scriptural evidence the harmony of the new message with the predictions of earlier times; expounding the truths embodied in the first principles of the Gospel; then if he bears his testimony under divine inspiration, such a testimony is as a seal attesting the genuineness of the truths he has declared, and so appealing to the receptive soul whose ears have been saluted by the heaven-sent message. (*Joseph F. Smith*, JI, 1 Aug. 1906, p. 465.)

(11A-7) *Nurturing your own seed.* You don't get a testimony of the gospel through your father's and mother's testimony or through your neighbor's. You have a seed planted in your hearts, in your souls, in your minds, and it is good and tastes good and feels good to you. And then, as it feels good and you harbor it and nurture it and want to expand, you will seek out things which corroborate and give you the same feeling. And the whispering of the Holy Ghost in that manner will bring it to you until you have assurance that you are not only on the right track, but you have found the truth. It comes as simply as that. And truly the Lord spoke rightly when he said that it is the kind of thing that a wayfaring man though a fool need not err therein. It doesn't require erudition; it doesn't require education, as valuable as that may be. It requires simple faith — a simple desire to nurture the seeds which are borne into your souls and to find the truth thereof, by continuing until they come full bloom. (S. *Dilworth Young*, BYU, 10 Dec. 1968, p. 11.)

B. Others May Draw Strength from Your Testimony

(11B-1) *People are fed when they hear testimony borne.* Paul said, "Our gospel came not unto you in word only, but also in power, and in the Holy Ghost, and in much assurance." (1 Thessalonians 1:5.) "Much assurance," what is that? Well, it is much testimony. It is repeated assertions that the work is true. If there is anything (and there are lots of things) that sets us apart from the world, it is this matter of testimony bearing. We set up a schedule, we have a program so that we have a formal testimony meeting once a month in every ward and every branch of the Church. People are fed the bread of life when they hear testimony borne. (*Bruce R. McConkie*, ACR, Feb. 1976 — Sydney, Australia, p. 21.)

(11B-2) *To assist in strengthening the testimonies of others.* When we bear testimony we are teaching others the truths that have enriched our lives and made us happy. Our testimonies are borne — First, to give thanks to God for the knowledge and assurances he has given us; second, to assist our brethren and sisters in the strengthening of their testimonies; and third, to carry the conviction which is ours into the hearts of all other people upon the face of the earth. (*Henry D. Moyle*, CR, Apr. 1957, p. 32.)

(11B-3) *Cling to my testimony until you develop one for yourself.* Sometimes as I go into the mission field I find a young man who says to me, "I don't have a testimony." My reply, "My boy, let me bear you my testimony, and for the time being suppose you cling to my testimony until you develop one for yourself." That is what I am saying to you young people today. Maybe you haven't developed to maturity your testimony. To give you that strength and resistance and until you develop one for yourself, then hold on to those of ours until you can develop one for yourselves. . . .

How I wish I could impress you who must daily walk out on the swaying bridge of worldliness and sin which flows as a turbulent stream below you, how I wish that when you have twinges of doubt and fear that cause you to lose the rhythm of prayer and faith and love, may you hear my voice as one calling to you from further along on life's bridge. "Have faith — this is the way — for I can see further ahead than you." I would fervently pray that you could feel the love flowing from my soul to yours, and know of my deep compassion toward each of you as you face your problems of the day. (*Harold B. Lee*, DSL, pp. 226, 234.)

(11B-4) *Bear your testimony so that they may have something to cling to.* I . . . bear my solemn testimony to you who may be wavering, and who haven't developed a testimony. I know that this is the Lord's work. I know that Jesus Christ lives, and that He is closer to this Church, and appears more often in holy places than any of us realize, excepting sometimes to those to whom he makes personal appearance. I know it, and the time is hastening when he shall come again to reign as Lord of Lords and King of Kings. You leaders, you have young people who don't have that faith and that testimony, but don't neglect to bear your testimony to them so that they may have something to cling to, when turmoil comes in their lives, and the temptations and the fires of Satan are burning hot in their lives. (*Harold B. Lee*, UA-CHD, 29 June 1969 — Salt Lake City, Utah, pp. 9-10.)

(11B-5) *It strengthens the testimonies of other people.* We are a testimony-bearing people. Everywhere and always in our meetings somebody is saying, "I know that the work is true." This is sound and this is good; this is the way things ought to be. We ought to bear testimony nearly all the time, because when we bear testimony it strengthens the testimonies of other people. If we get the Spirit of the Lord in our soul, and certify by the power of the Holy Ghost that the work is true, then everybody that hears us who is in tune with the same Spirit knows also in his heart that the work is true. (*Bruce R. McConkie*, BYU, 11 Feb. 1968, p. 11.)

(11B-6) *The gift of being thrilled by their testimony.* Now may we reiterate the most important and precious gift of all. That gift is cited in Section 46, verse 13: "To some it is given by the Holy Ghost to know that Jesus Christ is the Son of God, and that he was crucified for the sins of the world."

This is the most precious of all gifts — *to know that Jesus is the Christ.* With that sure knowledge, our lives are tempered, always in the right direction, as we seek to gain the perfection that will one day bring us into His holy presence.

Then it goes on to say: "To others it is given to believe on their words, . . ." (Doctrine and Covenants 46:14) — on the words of those who can proclaim that they *know* that Jesus is the Christ. So as these men who have been appointed and ordained as prophets, seers, and revelators look you squarely in the eye and say, "I know that God lives, I know that Jesus is the Christ!" so you, too, if you have not arrived at that point, can have the *gift of being thrilled by their testimony and believing* to a large degree yourselves, preparatory to having that sure knowledge which will come with time and proper effort. (*Robert L. Simpson,* BYU, 18 Oct. 1966, pp. 6-7.)

(11B-7) *There must be some influence that touches their lives.* I have a friend who once was called into a court as a juryman. Before the trial he knew nothing about the character of the evidence but he was acquainted with the prisoner at the bar. Most certainly this prisoner could not be guilty of the things charged. He would stake his life on that. The trial opened; the evidence was unfolded link by link. The farther it progressed the more astonished my friend became. In the end he voted for conviction. The evidence was overwhelming. His belief in innocence changed to a certainty of guilt. It was the testimony of reputable witnesses that produced the change. And so my doubting friend, look about you. Do you know any reputable people who declare that they know that God lives? Do you know any others whose lives are so saint-like that they are radiant with sunshine and whose very presence is a benediction? Well, does not the fact that there are such people lead you to believe that there must be some influence that touches their lives and not yours? (*Joseph F. Merrill,* CN, 22 Sept. 1945, p. 12.)

C. God's Way of Building the Church: Individual Conversion

(11C-1) *"The Mormon Church is my true church"* emblazoned across the heavens. As we contemplate people coming into this church and being interested in the message that we have, wouldn't it be a simple matter for Heavenly Father to take the missionary effort into his own hands.

He has created heaven and earth, he knows all about everything that there is. It would be such a simple thing for him to just emblazon across the heavens tonight in great big neon letters (or anything else that would be appropriate), "THE MORMON CHURCH IS MY TRUE CHURCH." He could just put that right across the heavens and we would really pack them in next Sunday, wouldn't we? We'd have people out on the parking lots. We'd have people come by the thousands.

There's only one thing wrong with that plan. A week from Saturday night they would be out looking for another miracle to see if they had to go to church again tomorrow. If people come into this church through a miracle, it's a miracle if they stay in the church. And so, Heavenly Father decided a long time ago that people would come into this church as they are convinced on a person-to-person basis; and that's why we have more than seventeen thousand missionaries out in the world, bearing testimony, seeking out the honest in heart, taking time to explain these concepts that are so vital to the success and happiness of mankind.

Wouldn't it be a simple thing for the Savior, if he so decided, to direct the Prophet to put a large video screen up in the front of every chapel? The Savior of the world, through closed-circuit television (which we've perfected) could give the major address at every Sacrament Meeting in the church; small video screens in every classroom, and the Master could teach all the Primary children, he could teach all the MIA people, he could teach every Sunday School class. The Master Teacher, teaching with perfection, convincing and converting, and putting all of us out of our teaching assignment. This would of course block our progress and keep us from achieving all that the Lord has in mind for us. (*Robert L. Simpson*, UU, 2 Nov. 1973, pp. 6-7.)

(11C-2) *Joining the Church as a business proposition.* I was once conversing with a gentleman who expressed an earnest desire that the Latter-day Saints should cooperate with those rich philanthropists who are endeavoring to colonize the poor Jews of Christian countries — to move them out of the large cities — to make farmers and artisans of a people who have been peddlers, merchants, and money changers for centuries. One of these colonies, by the way, is in central Utah, near the town of Gunnison. This gentleman said to me, "I recognize the 'Mormon' people as the greatest colonizers in the world, and I wonder why you don't see the necessity of cooperating with such men as Baron Hirsch, who has spent millions of wealth endeavoring to colonize these Jews, but has failed thus far, because of his lack of knowledge and experience in colonizing methods. Why don't you Latter-day Saints cooperate with him, he to provide the millions, you to furnish the experience?" And he added, "You could make a stipulation that every Jew you helped to colonize should become a Latter-day Saint." [Laughter.] "See how that would build up your Church."

I answered Mr. Davenport — that was the gentleman's name — in substance as follows: "You remind me of a conversion I once had in the Eastern States, while upon my first mission. I was asked, "Why don't you 'Mormon' elders fly for higher game? Why do you always preach to the poor and the lowly? Why don't you get up among the high and the mighty? Take Henry Ward Beecher, for instance" — he was then alive, the great pastor of the Brooklyn Tabernacle — "convert him and his whole congregation would flock in after him; and just see how that would build up your Church!" I said to Mr. Davenport, "That is not God's way of building up His church. The Lord declared by an ancient prophet, 'I will take you one of a city and two of a family, and I will bring you to Zion and give you pastors after mine own heart.' " I explained the great problem of the dispersion and gathering of Israel, whereby the blood of Abraham, Isaac and Jacob, the blood that believes, with spirits answering to that blood, who have been dispersed for a wise purpose among all nations, are now being recalled and brought together in a great movement called "The Gathering," preparatory to the building of the New Jerusalem and the glorious coming of the Lord. And I added, "God is not anxious for great congregations. He is not desirous that the Jews, or any other people, should make a bargain with Him and join His Church as a business proposition." . . . Christians are not made by judicial decisions, nor are Latter-day Saints converted by legislative enactment or by commercial bargaining. (*Orson F. Whitney*, CR, Apr. 1914, pp. 42-43.)

12

PARENTS AND THEIR CHILDREN'S TESTIMONIES

A.   No One Is Born with a Testimony

(12A-1) *People are not born with a testimony.* Some people have the idea
that they are born with a testimony. I do not happen to believe that any
such thing as that takes place. I know that we are born with the blood of
Israel in us, which is believing blood, and I know that people have
believing hearts; but some have more believing tendencies in their souls
than do others. I also feel like Paul, "How shall they believe in him of
whom they have not heard?" Or to put it in the words of President
Heber J. Grant:

> It is folly to imagine that our children will grow up with a
> knowledge of the Gospel without teaching. Some men and
> women argue "Well, I am a Latter-day Saint and we were
> married in the Temple and were sealed over the altar by one
> having the Priesthood of God, according to the new and ever-
> lasting covenant, and our children are bound to grow up and be
> good Latter-day Saints; they cannot help it; it is born in them."
>
> I have learned the multiplication table, and so has my wife,
> but do you think I am big enough fool to believe that our
> children will be born with a knowledge of the multiplication
> table?

I may know the Gospel is true, and so may my wife, but I want to tell you that our children will not know the Gospel is true unless they study it and gain a testimony for themselves. Parents are deceiving themselves in imagining that their children will be born with a knowledge of the Gospel. (*Gospel Standards*, page 155.)

(*Mark E. Petersen, UA-CHD, 11 July 1956 — Provo, Utah, pp. 4-5.*)

(12A-2) *Do people born in the Church go through the same process?* How many who are born in the Church have testimonies of the truthfulness of the Gospel? It is true that the converts have testimonies, but what of the rest of us? Have we as sure a faith as the converts?

People who are converted to the Church through the work of our missionaries study the Gospel, read the scriptures, and seek out a knowledge of the truth for themselves. As they seek it, and pray for it, they obtain it.

But do people in the Church go through that same type of process, or do they take matters for granted?

Many homes do not have a program by which they teach their children the Gospel in the home. They depend entirely upon the auxiliary organizations to teach and train their children in the faith. The result is that at times some never really are taught, they never grasp the significance of their Church membership. And if they do not, can we say they are converted?

Just as a convert must study and pray for a knowledge of the truth, so must those who are born in the Church. . . . No matter how well established in the faith the parents may be, their children are not born with this same faith and testimony. They must acquire it, just as other people do. . . .

Every parent and every Church worker is or should be a preacher. In every home the Gospel should be taught and taught from the scriptures. Every child should be taught to love the scriptures, and profit by their instructions.

They can never have a testimony of the truthfulness of the Book of Mormon if they know nothing of it, if they never read it. They can never have a testimony of the Bible if they never read it, nor of the other standards works of the Church.

Instructors in the Church and parents in the home must join in a concerted effort to have the youth of the Church obtain intelligent testimonies of the truth. This must be done by proper instructions, and who can say that we can properly instruct anyone in the faith without the use and knowledge of the holy scriptures? (*Mark E. Petersen*, FL, pp. 330-331.)

B.   Responsibility of Helping Your Children "Know"

(12B-1) *You too must know, my son.* We have the responsibility not to deny our children, for whatever reason, the chance to learn from us those principles which form a foundation for whatever is good in us.

Those familiar with the scriptures are aware that many of the most powerful and personally helpful teachings of the sacred records are from parents to their own children, often from fathers to sons. . . .

One powerful and motivating example of a father's instructions to his children is the series of chapters in which Alma shares with his sons the profoundest lessons of his own life. From his experiences, good and bad (for he had both, like the rest of us), there were certain crucial convictions which he was anxious to teach. Of three such matters this humble man speaks in a strong and tender testimony to his son Helaman (Alma 36), and repeats the witness to his other children.

"My son," he said, "thou art in thy youth, and therefore, I beseech of thee that thou wilt hear my words and learn of me; for I do know that whosoever shall put their trust in God shall be supported in their trials, and their troubles, and their afflictions, and shall be lifted up at the last day. And I would not that ye think that I know of myself — not of the temporal but of the spiritual, not of the carnal mind but of God." (Alma 36:3-4.)

" . . . [for] it is the Spirit of God which is in me which maketh these things known unto me; for if I had not been born of God I should not have known these things. . . . and never, until I did cry out unto the Lord Jesus Christ for mercy, did I receive a remission of my sins. But . . . I did cry unto him and I did find peace to my soul." (Alma 38:6-8.)

"And I have been supported under trials and troubles of every kind, yea, and in all manner of afflictions; . . . and I do put my trust in him, and he will still deliver me." (Alma 36:27.)

"And now, my son, I have told you this that ye may learn wisdom, that ye may learn of me that there is no other way or means whereby man can be saved, only in and through Christ. Behold, he is the life and the light of the world. Behold, he is the word of truth and righteousness." (Alma 38:9.)

That was this father's first great witness to his sons: that he knew, in the only way men can know — that is, through the Spirit — that God lives, that Jesus is the Christ, and that through him the penitent can be born again.

There is a second matter of which Alma testified to his son — that from the time of his own witness from the Lord, he said, "I have labored without ceasing, that I might bring souls unto repentance; that I might bring them to taste of that exceeding joy of which I did taste; that they might also be born of God, and be filled with the Holy Ghost . . . . my son, the Lord doth give me exceeding great joy in the fruit of my labors; For because of the word which he has imparted unto me . . . many have been born of God, and have tasted as I have tasted, and have seen eye to eye as I have seen; therefore they do know of these things of which I have spoken, as I do know; and the knowledge which I have is of God." (Alma 36:24-26.)

Because he knew, many others had received the same blessing. He had become a willing and effective instrument in the hands of God to bring others to a knowledge of the truth.

But this was not enough for Alma, as indeed it is not for any man who has a witness by the Spirit and loves someone very much. Thus, he had a third vital message to deliver: "But behold, my son, this is not all; for ye ought to know as I do know." (Alma 36:30.)

Of course! It is not enough for any loving father that he has the witness himself, nor enough that he has helped others to gain a knowledge of true principles. He cannot be truly content unless those he loves best also know. It is with every true father as with Israel of old: "If I be bereaved of my children, I am bereaved." (Genesis 43:14.) And with Judah: "How shall I go up to my father, and the lad be not with me?" (Genesis 43:44.)

These, then, were the vital matters which Alma had to be sure his sons understood. He taught them many related truths, many wonderful principles, but none more important: He knew! Through the graciousness and mercy of God he knew!

Through him others had been taught. But this was not enough; his son too must know! That same testimony I bear today to my own son and daughters. I do know that God lives and that Jesus is the Christ. Because I know, some others have had a chance to learn.

But this is not enough, my children; you must know for yourselves. (*Marion D. Hanks*, CR, Oct. 1975, pp. 35-36.)

(12B-2) *It is the duty of the older members.* It is the duty of the older members, the fathers, uncles, grandfathers, cousins, and so forth, who have this testimony in their hearts, to establish it in the hearts of these growing young men, so that at such time as they may come to us and offer their services that they may have a living testimony that Christ is the Son of God, that the Church was authoritatively organized, that the priesthood is in the earth, all of which is essential to the exaltation of men. (*Antoine R. Ivins*, CR, Oct. 1958, p. 10.)

(12B-3) *Among our neighbors are those of our own households.* It is important now, as it has always been, that every man go to with his might, "take righteousness in his hands and faithfulness upon his loins, and lift a warning voice unto the inhabitants of the earth. . . ." (Doctrine and Covenants 63:37.)

". . . every man to his neighbor, in mildness and in meekness." (Doctrine and Covenants 38:41.)

And let each of us remember that among our neighbors are those of our own households who must know for themselves. (*Marion D. Hanks*, CR, Oct. 1975, p. 37.)

(12B-4) *Testimony best nurtured in the family setting.* A testimony is best nurtured in the family setting. Once nurtured, that testimony will be strengthened in the meetings of the Church, through study of the words of the prophets recorded in ancient and modern writings, and through doing the work of the Church. [Church magazines] . . . will be great aids to families in helping each member gain a testimony, for the gaining and keeping of testimonies should be a family project. Do not neglect anything that will help to strengthen the testimony of any member of your family. (*Joseph Fielding Smith*, IE, Nov. 1970, p. 11.)

(12B-5) *How many are showing our young people how . . .* But as I have listened to the testimonies that have been borne, I have often wondered how many of us are showing our young people *how* they may know, and if we are sufficiently emphasizing the fact that they will never gain a testimony if they indulge in sin; that they will never know if they live to gratify their passions and appetites. "My spirit shall not always strive with man." (Genesis 6:3; see Doctrine and Covenants 1:33; Moses 8:17.) His spirit will not dwell in unclean tabernacles. " . . . The Spirit of the Lord doth not dwell in unholy temples." (Helaman 4:24.) Do they know that one cannot have a testimony without the Spirit of God? (*David O. McKay*, IN, Mar. 1966, pp. 81-82.)

C.   Children Should Hear the Testimonies of Their Parents

(12C-1) *Testimony bearing among family members.* Every child that grows up in a Latter-day Saint home is entitled to hear his father and his mother say, "I know this work is true." How often do you bear testimony to your children? Do you have a family home evening and have a discussion and take occasion in the course of it to say just plainly and quietly and serenely and calmly that the work is true, that the Lord's hand is in it? Every wife in this Church is entitled to hear her husband say that he knows this work is true, and every husband in this Church is entitled to hear his wife say that she knows the work is true. (*Bruce R. McConkie*, ACR, Feb. 1976 — Sydney, Australia, p. 21.)

(12C-2) *How wise is the father or grandfather who bears his testimony.* Our children should hear, in the privacy of the home, the testimonies of their parents. How wise is the father or grandfather who takes occasion to bear his personal testimony to each of his children, individually. If we did our duty as parents and leaders, there are many such specific things we could do to bolster the home. (*Harold B. Lee*, UA-CHD, 3 Oct. 1968 — Salt Lake City, Utah, p. 13.)

(12C-3) *Father, did you share your testimony with your children?* Father, you are accountable to the Lord for what you have and what you are. In the future you will surely stand before him. What will be your report concerning your family? Will you be able to report that your home was a place of love, a bit of heaven? That daily family prayer and secret prayer were fostered? That it was a house of fasting? That in family home evenings and at other times you and your wife taught your children the basic principles of the gospel?

Will you be able to report that you created an environment in your home to build faith in a living God, to encourage learning, to teach order, obedience, and sacrifice? That you often shared your testimony of the reality of your Father in heaven, of the truthfulness of the restored gospel with your wife and children? Will you be able to report that you followed the living prophets? That your home was where your tender children could feel protected and safe, and where they felt the love, and acceptance, and warmth of you and their mother? (*Harold B. Lee,* FCW, pp. 3-4.)

(12C-4) *A mother's promise.* Did my father know that this was God's Church? I have heard him as well as my mother testify that they knew it. I believed them, but for years and years I could not say the same thing. Friends and brethren and sisters, one of the greatest blessings that ever came to me was the revelation of my Heavenly Father as to this work of His. I remember when my mother used to talk to me and say: "You may not have a testimony now, as you say you haven't, but I promise you as your mother that if you will keep yourself unspotted from the sins of this world, if you will ask in earnestness and sincerity and faith, your Heavenly Father for that testimony and live for it, as your mother I promise you you shall have that testimony."

Brethren and sisters, I testify that I do have it. It came as my mother said it would, and I want to promise you here today that if you seek God in earnestness, in prayer and in faith, asking that He manifest to you in some way that will inspire you with a knowledge that this is His Gospel, it will come in time. (*Reed Smoot,* CN, 7 Mar. 1936, p. 2.)

D.   Age No Factor in Gaining a Testimony

(12D-1) *Their knowledge is limited but they can have feelings.* I remember bearing my testimony when I was just a child in Primary and in Sunday School. It is basic. It is important. We have critics who say it is silly to have little children bear their testimonies and that they cannot know it is true. Undoubtedly their knowledge is limited. But they can have feelings, and testimonies are feelings, not merely the accumulation of facts. Testimonies come from the heart. (*Spencer W. Kimball,* UA-CHD, 15 Jan. 1962 — Berlin, Germany, p. 1.)

(12D-2) *You do not need to be old.* If you don't know the gospel's true, I advise you to find it out. You do not have to be old in order to know it. When you have gone down in the waters of baptism, and you have received the Holy Ghost, you can be entitled to the inspiration and the revelation of the Holy Ghost, and you do not need to be old in order to get that witness of the truth of the Church. (*LeGrand Richards,* BYU, 1972-1973, p. 39.)

(12D-3) *Young children and testimony.* At the fast meeting that was held after I had been confirmed a member of the Church a dear old auntie, who long since has gone home, asked me, "Don't you want to bear your testimony?" I had heard others bear their testimonies, but I had never thought of bearing mine. I arose to my feet and I was just as sure then that I belonged to the Church of the Lamb of God as I am today. I was only a child, and that brings to my attention the fact that the Lord has given to our people a commandment that we are to teach our children to pray and to walk uprightly before him. He has said that parents in Zion having children shall teach them the Gospel of Jesus Christ and faith in God, and see that they are baptized and have the hands of the servants of God laid upon their heads for the bestowal of the Holy Ghost when eight years of age. And if we as parents fail in this duty the sin will be upon our heads.

There are many people who have believed that it is not possible for children to understand at eight, but I stand here today as a witness that I had that understanding as far as it was possible for me as a child to know. (*George Albert Smith,* CR, Apr. 1935, p. 43.)

(12D-4) *They may both claim respect.* The learned and the unlearned, the youth and the veteran, the high and the humble, may bear such a testimony alike. Each one learns the truth through his own powers. To each one may come the conviction that truth is the substance of the gospel and its claims. The man, rich in learning and experience, may be able to marshall more evidences for his belief than the adolescent lad; but, since both have tested the gospel with the means at their command, and found it not wanting, they may both claim respect for their separate testimonies. (*John A. Widtsoe,* IE, May 1943, p. 289.)

✤13✤
TEACHERS AND THEIR STUDENTS' TESTIMONIES

A. The Importance of Bearing Testimony When Teaching

(13A-1) *The controlling factor in teaching.* We have something which no one else can have. The pope in Rome might be a good man. Some ministers and some priests may be righteous. Some might be as devoted and as sincere as we are. But, there can be none except in our Church, of course, who have this controlling thing, the testimony of the truth, and that is the thing that brings people into the Kingdom. It is not our logic. Some may be more adept than others, some may have more natural endowments and greater talents than others and some may be able to give a better lesson. But that is not the controlling factor, though it helps. It is tremendously important that we do everything in our power to present it well but the testimony is the sealing element. (*Spencer W. Kimball,* UA-CHD, 15 Jan. 1962 — Berlin, Germany, p. 1.)

(13A-2) *An approving divine seal on the doctrine we teach.* Now I do not minimize in any degree or to any extent the obligation that rests upon us to be gospel scholars, to search the revelations, to learn how to reason and analyze, to present the message of salvation among ourselves and to the world with all the power and ability we have; but that standing alone does not suffice. When that is all over, we have to comply with the command the Lord gave for us in this day: ". . . ye are my witnesses, saith the Lord, that I am God." (Isaiah 43:12.) We have to put an approving, divine seal on the doctrine that we teach and that seal is the seal of testimony, the seal of a personal knowledge borne of the Holy Ghost. . . .

Now how do you prove and establish that the Father and Son appeared to Joseph Smith; that angels came in our day; that there has been a restoration of the gospel; that all the glorious things we present to the world are true? Well, you reason out of the revelations. You can make a good case; and that isn't any problem. The truth is with us. The Lord is the author of the system we have received. But after you have reasoned and after you have analyzed, you have got to stand as a personal witness who knows what he is saying. You have to . . . speak and teach by the spirit of prophecy and the spirit of revelation; and the result is that you speak as one having authority. This is the great thing that separates us from the world, and thanks be to God we have this knowledge. We have received this revelation, and we are in a position to speak as those having authority. (*Bruce R. McConkie*, CR, Apr. 1973, pp. 36-37.)

(13A-3) *There is no need to try to justify, to equivocate, to rationalize.* I make a plea to all of you to try a little harder to breathe a little more of the spirit of testimony into all that you teach. Teach faith in God, the Father of us all, the Creator of the universe, a living, personal Being to whom we may go in prayer with full expectation that our prayers will be heard and answered according to His will and wisdom.

Teach faith in Jesus Christ, the Son of God, the Word that was made flesh and dwelt among us, the only perfect life that was ever lived, the Exemplar for all men, the Lamb who was sacrificed for the sins of the world, our Redeemer and our Savior.

There is no need to try to justify, to equivocate, to rationalize, to enlarge, to explain. Why should we equivocate? Why should we rationalize? I give you these great words of Paul to Timothy: "For God hath not given us the spirit of fear, but of power, and of love, and of a sound mind. Be not thou therefore ashamed of the testimony of our Lord." (2 Timothy 1:7-8.)

I wish every member of this institution would print that and put it on his mirror where he would see it every morning as he begins his day. "Be not thou therefore ashamed of the testimony of our Lord."

Teach the simple, straightforward truth that came out of the vision of the boy Joseph Smith. Teach the reality of that vision and the manifestations that followed, that brought into being the restored Church of Jesus Christ — The Church of Jesus Christ of Latter-day Saints.

The students have come to you to learn. Teach them these truths as facts, for so they are. (*Gordon B. Hinckley*, UA-CHD, 17 Sept. 1963 — Provo, Utah, p. 5.)

(13A-4) *Even the Lord bore testimony in teaching.* The testimony is basic. The Lord Himself recognized that. He bore His testimony of Himself and of His program. Do you remember when Nicodemus came at night, fearful, timid to get a little information from the Lord? He wanted to know something about Him and His work, and the Lord told him, "A man must be born again." Nicodemus could not understand. Then the Lord began to bear His testimony, after He had explained the gospel to Nicodemus. We have only a few verses, but I suspect that it may have been an interview lasting many minutes, or perhaps hours that night when this great educator came and stood in the presence of this humble Nazarene. I suspect it was a long interview, and then the Lord noticed the furrowed brows of this man who could not understand. He was an educated man, a highly trained man, but could not comprehend the simple things. He knew a great deal about academic subjects, I suppose, but he could not seem to understand this. The Lord was disappointed and He said: "Verily, verily, I say unto you, Except a man be born of the water and of the Spirit, he cannot enter into the kingdom of heaven." (John 3:5.)

This is hard for an intellectual to understand, unless he has the spirituality with it. Then the Lord said: ". . . Marvel not at this when I say you must be born again." Don't knit your furrows, Mr. Nicodemus, listen and open your heart and you will understand things you never could learn in books or in colleges. And then He says, "The wind bloweth where it listeth, and thou hearest the sound thereof, but canst not tell whence it cometh, and whither it goeth: so is every one that is born of the Spirit." (John 3:8.)

. . . There are people who pride themselves on their keen minds, who think they can delve into mysteries, but they can never define or explain or understand the spiritual things through their logic or through their mental processes. The spiritual things can be understood only through the Spirit. It must come through the heart and that is where the testimony is lodged. Then the Lord said to this man who could not understand the simple things, this highly educated man could understand complex problems, but this simple truth was beyond him, and the Lord said to him, "Art thou a master of Israel, and knowest not these things? Verily, verily [surely, surely, without question], I say unto thee, We speak that we do know, and testify that we have seen; and ye receive not our witness." (John 3:10, 11.)

He said in effect, "Nicodemus, I have borne my testimony to you, I, the Son of God, but you did not listen. You did not receive it." I quote His words: "If I have told you earthly things and ye believe not, how shall ye believe, if I tell you of heavenly things?" (John 3:12.)

That is His testimony. (*Spencer W. Kimball*, UA-CHD, 15 Jan. 1962 — Berlin, Germany, pp. 3-4.)

(13A-5) *We do two things: we teach and we testify.* We do two things: we teach and we testify. We have to teach first so that we will have a basis for a testimony. We don't just bear testimony promiscuously; we bear testimony to back up teaching. . . .

The more we can do by logic and sense and reason and scripture to lay this thing out for people, so much the better. But the final, concluding, crowning thing is the witness of the Spirit. (*Bruce R. McConkie*, ACR, Feb. 1976 — Sydney, Australia, pp. 19, 21.)

B. Qualifications for Gospel Teachers

(13B-1) *The first requisite of a teacher.* The first requisite of a teacher for teaching these principles is a personal testimony of the truth. No amount of learning, no amount of study, and no number of scholastic degrees, can take the place of this testimony, which is the *sine qua non* of the teacher. . . .

But for you teachers the mere possession of a testimony is not enough. You must have besides this, one of the rarest and most precious of all the many elements of human character — moral courage. For in the absence of moral courage to declare your testimony, it will reach the students only after such dilution as will make it difficult if not impossible for them to detect it; and the spiritual and psychological effect of a weak and vacillating testimony may well be actually harmful instead of helpful.

The successful . . . teacher must also possess another of the rare and valuable elements of character — a twin brother of moral courage and often mistaken for it — I mean intellectual courage — the courage to affirm principles, beliefs, and faith that may not always be considered as harmonizing with such knowledge — scientific or otherwise — as the teacher or his educational colleagues may believe they possess.

Not unknown are cases where men of presumed faith, holding responsible positions, have felt that, since by affirming their full faith they might call down upon themselves the ridicule of their unbelieving colleagues, they must either modify or explain away their faith, or destructively dilute it, or even pretend to cast it away. Such are hypocrites to their colleagues and to their co-religionists.

An object of pity (not of scorn, as some would have it) is that man or woman, who having the truth and knowing it, finds it necessary either to repudiate the truth or to compromise with error in order that he may live with or among unbelievers without subjecting himself to their disfavor or derision as he supposes. Tragic indeed is his place, for the real fact is that all such discardings and shadings in the end bring the very punishments that the weak-willed one sought to avoid. For there is nothing the world so values and reveres as the man, who, having righteous convictions, stands for them in any and all circumstances; there is nothing towards which the world turns more contempt than the man who, having righteous convictions, either slips away from them, abandons them, or repudiates them. (*J. Reuben Clark, Jr.*, IE, Sept. 1938, pp. 571-572.)

(13B-2) *Teachers are but little different from missionaries.* The bearing of sincere testimony is one of the most influential things a teacher can do before a class.

Testimony throughout the centuries has solved many problems and brought answers to many queries.

In courts of law testimony determines whether or not a person may be adjudged guilty of a crime. The testimony of archaeologists has altered the course of education in many respects. The testimony of scientists has been the basis of further exploration, even of the moon. Where would our present space program be without the testimony of the experts who have guided the project?

Testimony usually is based upon actual experience, either the personal witness of one who has seen a crime, or the experience of researching out data for a space probe, or the digging and dating processes of archaeologists, to mention a few examples.

How important is testimony in religion? And how vital is it in teaching religion?

New converts to the Church repeatedly say that one of the main factors in their conversion was the earnest testimony of the missionaries. And the testimony of the missionary is likewise based on experience — a spiritual experience which has convinced him of the truth of the Gospel himself and enabled him to tell others also that it is true.

Teachers in our organizations are but little different from missionaries. What they do in their classes is likewise a part of the teaching and conversion process for Latter-day Saints.

Teachers must convert those who come to their classes. They must do so by providing orthodox doctrine, by using good teaching methods, and certainly by bearing testimony — their own personal testimony.

President J. Reuben Clark, Jr., speaking on this subject at one time said this: "The first requisite of a teacher for teaching these principles is a personal testimony of the truth. No amount of learning, no amount of study, and no number of scholastic degrees can take the place of this testimony." (*Mark E. Petersen,* CN, 1 Nov. 1969, p. 16.)

(13B-3) *Living what you teach.* It is not what you eat that benefits you, but what you digest. What you hear today is of no use to you unless you put it into practice. Somebody has said, and I have often repeated it: "Knowledge without practice is like a glass eye — all for show and nothing for use.". . .

Knowledge is of no value unless you put it into practice. All the teachings in the world, unless the individual is living that which he teaches, will not carry the spirit of right action. It does not carry with it the weight; it does not really touch the hearts of those who listen. (*Heber J. Grant,* IE, Feb. 1933, p. 224.)

(13B-4) *Do we tarry occasionally?* You will recall that when the disciples were with the Master, and as he was about to leave them, knowing them to be human, knowing them to have their faults and their failings, knowing that he was leaving them to be the shepherds of the fold, he said to them, "Tarry ye at Jerusalem until the Comforter comes. I will send the Comforter, the Holy Ghost, and he will teach you all things."

Do we as teachers tarry once in a while to get the impress of the Comforter, to get inspiration from the Holy Ghost? That is important. We cannot be shepherds of the fold unless we have the gift of the Holy Ghost, its enlightenment; its inspiration. And if we have that gift, and if we tarry occasionally to get it when we feel that we have lost it, it will come — and then we will not take any liberty which will be a stumbling block to them that are weak. (*Matthew Cowley*, IN, Apr. 1952, p. 101.)

(13B-5) *Lip service is not sufficient.* I am convinced that all teachers need a burning testimony that this is God's work, the same as the convert in the missionary field must have, and we appeal to you workers to bring into all our various programs greater spirituality, for "the letter killeth, but the spirit giveth life." No matter how much these programs bring to you, they are the letter after all, and you teachers and leaders must furnish the spirit.

Your lip service is not sufficient; you must do more than that. The Lord has told us we shall not teach unless we teach under the influence of the Spirit. The gift and power of the Holy Ghost which is your right to enjoy should be your companion when you teach. (*Melvin J. Ballard*, MJB, p. 111.)

(13B-6) *Lest what we do know is called into question.* We must not let our tongues testify beyond what we know, lest what we do know is then called into question. Paul warned Timothy that some church members had swerved aside into "vain jangling" because, apparently, they desired "to be teachers of the law; understanding neither what they say, nor whereof they affirm." (1 Timothy 1:6-7.) Likewise, we must be careful not to let our desire to help give way under the temptation to have ready answers for everything. We must learn to endure sensitively when certain answers are not now available. (*Neal A. Maxwell*, WPF, p. 118.)

C. Those Who Tamper with Another's Testimony

(13C-1) *Tampering with a testimony.* This testimony is acquired by many with difficulty. I suppose that we often wish that it could be more easily obtained, and that it would come more generally to the people of the world, but God in his providence has made it somewhat difficult of attainment. Being so difficult to acquire, it seems to me to be a very serious thing to place one obstacle in the way of its attainment. I have wondered how it is that men who profess great learning and intelligence can throw an obstacle into the way of him who seeks the acquisition of this testimony. It may be that it is often done innocently. It may be that those who destroy faith are not fully aware of the consequences of their acts. If it be so, I trust God will be merciful to them, but I cannot think but that the Lord will hold responsible any man or woman who has increased the difficulty of another to obtain this light, this testimony of the divinity of Jesus Christ.

It is a matter of great regret that in our schools and colleges there are those who pass under the designation of educated men and women, who seem to rejoice in the destruction of the testimony and the faith of young people. I warn them that a persistence on their part to destroy faith and to keep this great thing we call testimony from reaching the hearts of students, young men and young women, will constitute an offense in the sight of God for which they shall be held accountable. (*Stephen L Richards,* CR, Oct. 1925, p. 120.)

(13C-2) *Leaders, do nothing to cause youth to doubt.* No bishop, no counselor, no stake president, no man holding a responsible position in this Church can afford to sidestep to the slightest degree his great responsibility of living the gospel as he preaches it and of being an example to the flock. Any man holding such a position who would lead a young person to doubt the Church by his actions will bring dishonor to the Church and great sorrow to his own soul. (*David O. McKay,* CR, Oct. 1968, p. 84.)

AUTHOR INDEX

Ashton, Marvin O.   (8D-6) Is your nest well feathered?

Ballard, Melvin J.   (13B-5) Lip service is not sufficient.

Brown, Hugh B.   (1A-4) A motivating, soul-transforming conviction; (1A-13) Commitment to a course of conduct; (3B-5) Prerequisites for a testimony; (5A-13) Statements of others should be confirmed by the Spirit; (8A-5) If we are not growing, we are dying; (8E-1) A testimony is gradually lost; (9A-5) Our lives must confirm our words.

Burton, Theodore M.   (3C-6) Our manner of life must change; (7A-5) Anything a person can be reasoned into, he can be reasoned out of; (9D-4) There is a difference between being convinced and converted.

Callis, Charles A.   (1A-9) Heart-knowledge, the strongest and most direct evidence of truth; (2B-7) Eternal hope and a heavenly monitor; (4C-4) Adversity and a testimony; (8E-11) Neglect of duty cuts off the channel of communication.

Cannon, Abraham H.   (3D-2) It is to him that you should appeal; (4A-4) It may not come in the way we desire; (5A-9) They do not dig down to the root of things.

Cannon, George Q.   (3E-1) Lack of this knowledge indicates slothfulness and laxness; (7A-13) A rash and ill-considered statement.

Clark, J. Reuben, Jr.   (1A-11) The thing which gives us power to endure; (1A-14) A sacred gift; (3A-6) May you not be content with just one experiment; (4A-5) The type of testimony the Lord blessed; (5A-3) It could be a bad thing for us to depend on others; (13B-1) The first requisite of a teacher; (13B-2) quoted by Mark E. Petersen.

Cowley, Matthew   (13B-4) Do we tarry occasionally?

Dunn, Loren C.   (3C-3) A three-month experiment; (3E-4) The error is in doing nothing about it; (4A-6) More than likely it will come in a rather calm, natural but real way; (4B-5) The witness of the Spirit is still necessary; (4C-2)

People who do not know that they know; (4D-7) A knowledge of God does not come instantaneously; (6A-5) You shall feel that it is right; (7C-2) You haven't been in the Church yet; (7C-4) "Two churches" within the Church; (8C-11) Vitality of a testimony maintained by participation; (8D-8) In preparation for the Second Coming, examine your testimony; (9A-1) Some people hear the words, some people understand; (10A-4) Something more than a passing reference.

Dunn, Paul H.   (3D-5) They too deserve an honest hearing.

Dyer, Alvin R.   (1A-8) The power that binds man and God together; (8C-9) He who adds not lacks power to maintain; (8D-3) Are you borrowing from bygone inspiration? (10A-5) Crying while bearing testimony.

Grant, Heber J.   (3B-13) And yet the spirit of God will not burn in their hearts; (3C-4) To those who would give everything they have for a testimony; (4A-10) Do you expect the Lord to get a club and knock you down? (4B-2) quoted by Harold B. Lee; (8D-5) quoted by John Longden; (8E-5) That doesn't amount to anything; (8E-8) Destroying their opportunities to grow; (12A-1) quoted by Mark E. Petersen; (13B-3) Living what you teach.

Hanks, Marion D.   (7A-4) When the light rested upon me I saw . . . ; (7A-7) Unless the Spirit of God carries the message the truth will never be understood; (12B-1) You too must know, my son; (12B-3) Among our neighbors are those of our own households.

Hinckley, Gordon B.   (2A-2) Strength of the Church not in its buildings, chapels, etc.; (2B-6) Requirements become challenges rather than burdens; (3B-4) They must be able to bend in humility; (3B-6) Three rules for acquisition of spiritual knowledge; (7A-8) Many of us have the same problem that Nicodemus had; (8B-7) When there beat in your hearts a witness and a testimony; (13A-3) There is no need to try to justify, to equivocate, to rationalize.

Hunter, Howard W.   (3C-7) Action is one of the chief foundations of personal testimony; (4C-3) Many people do not recognize that they carry a testimony.

Hunter, Milton R.   (1A-6) A divine power which lights up men's souls; (2A-4) It was not Brigham Young; (6A-3) On rare and marvelous occasions.

Isaacson, Thorpe B.   (4D-2) The full-bloom rose was once an unopened bud;

(8B-2) A testimony needs to be constantly reinforced; (8F-2) When your testimony is waning.

Ivins, Antoine R. (12B-2) It is the duty of the older members.

Kimball, Heber C. (5A-5) quoted by Robert L. Simpson; (5B-3) quoted by Harold B. Lee; (5B-5) quoted by J. Golden Kimball; (5B-7) quoted by J. Golden Kimball; (6A-3) quoted by Milton R. Hunter.

Kimball, J. Golden (5B-5) And who will be able to stand? (5B-7) A testimony strong enough to withstand the test; (6A-4) I have felt that thrill.

Kimball, Spencer W. (1A-1) The power equipment removing boulders from the road; (1A-10) A personal revelation from God; (3A-1) It is obtained by intense strivings; (3A-7) An all-out effort is required; (3B-1) You must place yourself in a proper frame of mind; (3C-8) Why are some so sure while others are passive? (3D-4) He is not found in a campus laboratory; (4C-1) It may be only "this" big; (6A-1) He cannot measure, weigh or count it; (7A-2) You must go to the spiritual laboratory; (7A-9) God cannot be found through research alone; (7B-2) The importance of spiritual knowledge; (7D-2) Placing unwarranted limitations on another's power; (8C-1) Like a muscle it grows stronger with use; (8C-8) Expressing our testimonies through service; (8C-10) To hold it, one must bear it often; (8E-4) A sure way to bring an end to one's testimony; (8E-6) He wondered why his spirit was dead; (8E-9) Spiritually cold and numb; (10A-1) Don't preach a sermon; (10A-2) Just tell how you feel; (10A-5) quoted by Alvin R. Dyer; (10B-1) Don't you ever worry about triteness; (10B-2) There are no words like "I know"; (10D-1) Testimony meetings are necessary at all levels; (10D-2) If you are bored there is something the matter with you; (10D-5) No one has had too many opportunities; (12D-1) Their knowledge is limited but they can have feelings; (13A-1) The controlling factor in teaching; (13A-4) Even the Lord bore testimony in teaching.

Lee, Harold B. (2A-7) The strength of the Church not in money paid as tithing; (3B-2) Important steps in gaining a testimony; (3B-7) Wrapping ourselves in obedience; (3C-9) Worthiness is essential to receive direction and guidance; (4A-2) When your heart tells you things your mind does not know; (4B-2) More important than sight is the witness of the Spirit; (5A-11) Too much confidence in the testimonies of others; (5B-1) The time is here to stand on your own feet; (5B-3) To be prepared for the millennial reign; (7B-1) We must keep spiritual and intellectual in balance; (7B-3) An expert in the spiritual field; (8A-2) It is as hard to hold as a moonbeam; (8A-4) Testimony of

today will not be the testimony of tomorrow; (8B-4) A testimony will grow dim
if not nourished; (8B-5) quoted by Henry D. Taylor; (9A-9) A truth is not a
truth until you live it; (9D-3) Measure of true conversion; (10C-2) They have
their own reward; (11A-2) It has to come from your own searching; (11B-3)
Cling to my testimony until you develop one for yourself; (11B-4) Bear your
testimony so that they may have something to cling to; (12C-2) How wise is
the father or grandfather who bears his testimony; (12C-3) Father, did you
share your testimony with your children?

Longden, John   (6A-2) I can feel just as good as anybody else; (8D-4) No
testimony is too strong.

Lund, Anthon H.   (8E-10) As long as you perform your duty.

Lyman, Francis M.   (3E-2) If they have lacked that witness it is their fault;
(5B-10) Help in time of trials.

Maxwell, Neal A.   (4A-8) A stupor or a burning are not the only ways in
which God can tell us; (8B-3) Do not neglect to nourish that tree by searching
the scriptures regularly; (8D-2) Are you receiving sufficient incoming experiences? (10D-7) One does not need perpetual reasons for re-entry; (13B-6) Lest
what we do know is called into question.

McConkie, Bruce R.   (1B-2) We mean three things in particular; (2B-5) A
testimony leads to revelation in other fields; (3B-12) How a knowledge of the
truth is obtained; (5A-4) To know for ourselves, independent of others; (6C-2)
Those who developed the talent for spirituality; (7A-1) A mental conviction is
only preparatory; (7A-10) Then he knows what the world does not know;
(7C-1) Identifying spiritually endowed people; (7C-3) What counts is to
become a personal participant; (7D-4) If I bear such a witness, it stands against
them; (7D-6) One of the wonders and the glories and the beauties of a
testimony; (8D-5) A testimony must be brought up to date to include the living
prophet; (8D-7) Are we perfecting our testimonies? (9B-1) Every member has
covenanted to be a witness; (9B-3) Three ways in which we bear testimony;
(9C-1) Lukewarm members of the Church are not valiant; (9C-2) To be
valiant in the testimony of Jesus is to . . . ; (9D-1) The process of conversion;
(11B-1) People are fed when they hear testimony borne; (11B-5) It
strengthens the testimonies of other people; (12C-1) Testimony bearing
among family members; (13A-2) An approving divine seal on the doctrine
we teach; (13A-5) We do two things: we teach and we testify.

McKay, David O. (1A-5) An anchor to the soul in the midst of confusion and strife; (2A-5) Wherein lies the secret of the Church's vitality? (2B-3) It enables one to pass through the dark valley of slander; (2C-7) The most useful possession in life; (3B-9) Introducing it into your very being; (4A-3) Physical manifestations are not the only source of testimony; (4A-7) Revelation, not miracles, should be the base for a testimony; (9A-8) The ability to live up to it; (12B-5) How many are showing our young people how . . . ? (13C-2) Leaders, do nothing to cause youth to doubt.

Merrill, Joseph F. (3A-4) Time and effort are necessary for the task; (7D-3) The testimony of a single witness with the facts; (9A-4) Because we know, we are bound; (11B-7) There must be some influence that touches their lives.

Moyle, Henry D. (7A-15) We must know our own spiritual senses; (11B-2) To assist in strengthening the testimonies of others.

Penrose, Charles W. (7A-12) An unlettered person enlightened direct from God will know more; (7A-14) Spiritual light versus natural light.

Petersen, Mark E. (1B-3) The mighty facts of which we bear testimony; (3B-11) That one experience was worth more than all the theories that men have produced; (4D-6) A testimony of the gospel is a composite of many testimonies; (8E-2) There is some "softening up" first; (9A-2) A testimony watered down by disobedience; (12A-1) People are not born with a testimony; (12A-2) Do people born in the Church go through the same process? (13B-2) Teachers are but little different from missionaries.

Rector, Hartman, Jr. (9D-2) A testimony and faith are not always synonymous; (10A-3) Statements of public thanks.

Richards, Franklin D. (3B-14) This formula when followed will bring a conviction; (8A-3) A testimony is never static.

Richards, LeGrand (2A-3) "Black secret" of Mormonism; (2B-2) Walking above the things of the world; (2C-3) The most valuable thing in the world; (2C-8) Greater than anything else achievable in life; (12D-2) You do not need to be old.

Richards, Stephen L (1A-2) An antitoxin against sin; (1A-7) A real and tangible transforming force; (1A-12) The greatest comfort that can come to a human heart; (2A-6) The Church is built on testimony; (6C-1) Some blood strains are more susceptible; (7D-1) Is a testimony susceptible to proof? (7D-7) Scientific knowledge versus spiritual knowledge; (9B-4) quoted by Marion G. Romney; (13C-1) Tampering with a testimony.

Romney, Marion G.   (1A-3) Key to successful living in all stages of existence; (1B-1) Aspects of a living testimony; (2C-1) The most precious of all possessions; (3C-1) Unless it is merited it will not come; (3D-1) You will never get a testimony by reading public magazines; (3F-3) There are not two ways, only one way; (4A-9) It is not easy to explain to the uninitiated; (4D-1) A testimony may come by degrees; (8F-1) Characteristics associated with a mature testimony; (9B-4) One cannot thereafter remain passive.

Simpson, Robert L.   (3C-2) Teach me all that I must do; (3D-3) So why not go directly to God? (3F-4) A gift for everyone, not just a select few; (5A-5) Standing upon our own two feet, spiritually speaking; (5A-7) We need to mature beyond that point; (8C-2) God's ways are not man's ways; (8C-6) Your testimony must be shared to survive; (9B-2) There is someone your testimony will appeal to; (10B-3) Even a counterfeit person could say "I know"; (11B-6) The gift of being thrilled by their testimony; (11C-1) "The Mormon Church is my true church" emblazoned across the heavens.

Smith, Eldred G.   (2C-2) A possession more valuable than sight; (3A-5) Study, pray, act — do something about it! (3B-10) How does one receive a message from the Holy Ghost? (4B-6) We can always trust spiritual promptings.

Smith, George Albert   (3E-5) Failure in our method; (12D-3) Young children and testimony.

Smith, John Henry   (3B-16) quoted by Delbert L. Stapley.

Smith, Joseph, Jr.   (3B-14) quoted by Franklin D. Richards; (4D-5) Spiritual knowledge will come one step at a time; (5A-4) quoted by Bruce R. McConkie; (7B-3) quoted by Harold B. Lee; (8F-1) quoted by Marion G. Romney; (10B-4) quoted by Robert L. Simpson.

Smith, Joseph F.   (2C-5) More valuable than mortal life; (4D-3) Little by little it will be obtained; (5A-2) A testimony so strong that when mortals fall you do not; (5A-8) A testimony of temporal as well as spiritual things; (5A-12) A fault to be avoided: living on borrowed light; (5B-9) Deep-rooted conviction necessary for the trials; (6A-6) I feel it in my soul — my whole being; (6A-7) He has made me to feel it; (8B-6) If neglected, it will not remain; (9A-3) Ready and willing to do the will of the Lord; (9A-7) If we know the truth — we must do right; (10A-6) Testimony not to be used to "fill up time"; (10D-3) Cultivation of feelings of gratitude; (10D-6) A source of help and encouragement; (11A-3) Impossible for me to know for you; (11A-4) He can touch your understanding: I cannot; (11A-6) One cannot give his testimony to another.

Smith, Joseph Fielding   (2C-6) Worth more than any sign or gift; (3C-5) Many members have not received because they fail to conform; (3C-10) The Holy Ghost will not dwell with the disobedient; (3E-3) We have no one to blame except ourselves; (4B-1) quoted by Henry D. Taylor; (4B-3) A witness far greater than seeing the Lord; (5A-6) That person has not lived up to his or her requirements; (12B-4) Testimony best nurtured in the family setting.

Smoot, Reed   (2C-4) I wanted every senator to know; (12C-4) A mother's promise.

Snow, Lorenzo   (4D-4) Pretty soon he is nearing the top of the mountain; (5B-2) Withstanding the tide of trouble; (5B-4) No man should be satisfied until he has secured a perfect assurance; (8C-5) He will receive continual additions.

Stapley, Delbert L.   (1B-4) Three important truths in every effective testimony; (2B-1) The fruits of a true testimony: high ideals; (2B-4) A shield against the fiery darts of the adversary; (3B-16) Live by faith first, then knowledge comes; (9A-6) The obligation to serve God.

Stone, O. Leslie   (3A-2) The Lord intended that we should work; (3F-2) It cannot be purchased; (8C-4) Things to do to strengthen a testimony; (9C-3) A testimony does not guarantee the celestial kingdom.

Talmage, James E.   (2A-1) This is the secret; (11A-1) No man can convert another; (11A-5) No testimonies to sell.

Taylor, Henry D.   (4B-1) The impressions made by the Holy Ghost can be equally deep and lasting; (8B-5) There is no guarantee that this testimony will remain steadfast.

Taylor, John   (7A-3) The limitations of earthly philosophies.

Vandenberg, John H.   (3A-3) It comes only after you have "hungered and thirsted" for it; (3B-15) The way to obtain a testimony is clear; (4A-1) It need not be a dramatic, emotional event.

Whitney, Orson F.   (2A-8) We are only a handful: testimony is our strength; (3F-1) Rules for a testimony the same regardless of learning; (4B-4) The greatest kind of testimony; (4C-5) Spiritual gold mines: latent and undeveloped; (5B-8) We will be tried to the very core; (7A-11) Blazing a trail, and marking out the way; (11C-2) Joining the Church as a business proposition.

Widtsoe, John A.   (1A-15) The highest type of knowledge; (3B-3) Specifically, what must a person do? (3B-8) The foundation for the search; (3C-11) They must test the principles; (5A-1) Superficial knowledge; (7D-5) Their method is without honor; (8A-1) It is much like a living thing; (8B-1) A testimony must be fed, cared for and nurtured; (8C-3) How may a testimony be kept? (8C-7) Formula for growth; (8D-1) Examine your weapon before the battle; (8E-3) How may a testimony be lost? (8E-7) Those who think they have "outgrown" a testimony; (10C-1) Not for the Church as a whole; (12D-4) They both claim respect.

Woodruff, Abraham O.   (9B-5) Obligation to make testimony known; (10D-4) I feel that the Lord is not pleased.

Woodruff, Wilford   (4B-7) There is no greater testimony given to man.

Young, Brigham   (3C-3) quoted by Loren C. Dunn; (5A-10) No man should trust solely the testimony of another; (5A-11) quoted by Harold B. Lee; (8E-7) quoted by John A. Widtsoe; (8F-1) quoted by Marion G. Romney; (9B-6) Be not miserly in your feelings.

Young, S. Dilworth   (5B-6) The only thing that will keep you in the Church; (6B-1) The greatest, most thrilling, most joyful earthly experience; (6B-2) Each of us is a Helen Keller in one way; (6B-3) The Spirit is more anxious to help us than we are to be helped; (7A-6) It does not come from preparation in earthly things; (11A-7) Nurturing your own seed.